The Water and the Blood, the Blood and the Water

Amelia K. Fulbright

The Water and the Blood, the Blood and the Water

Copyright © 2024 by Amelia K. Fulbright

All rights reserved.

No part of this book may be reproduced in any form or by any electronic or mechanical means, including information storage and retrieval systems, without written permission from the author, except for the use of brief quotations in a book review.

Tehom Center Publishing is a 501(c)3 non-profit imprint publishing feminist and queer authors, with a commitment to elevate BIPOC writers. Its face and voice is Rev. Dr. Angela Yarber.

Paperback ISBN: 978-1-966655-02-2

eBook ISBN: 978-1-966655-11-4

Contents

Holy Trinity: An Invocation	vii
1. The Water & the Blood: Preliminary Thoughts	1
2. The Mumbi, age 6	5
3. How I Learned Racism, age 8	9
4. Shaka Zulu, age 11	13
5. Early Signs of OCD	19
6. Therapy	21
7. Boys Outside the Bandroom	27
8. Testing the Bonds	33
9. Who Would Jesus Divorce?	37
10. Hacky Sack Boys	45
11. The Wreck	49
12. Divine Child Abuse	53
13. Observing Silence	57
14. This Flood	63
15. Queen City Mental Health	65
16. Alternative Medicines	73
17. White Weave	77
18. What Makes You a Whore	85
19. The Pulse	93
20. Tangled Roots	95
21. Born For Free	99
22. The World House	105
23. Risking Arrest	115
24. Behold, a Son!	123
25. 7 Centimeters	127
26. Foothills & Copper Belts: Mining for Kinship	133
27. Seven Layer Shame Cake	139

28. Why Don't You Know? 153
29. This Fragile White Woman's Tears 157
30. Mosi-oa-tunya (The Falls) 165
31. Why I Am Writing This Now 171
32. Upstream 179
33. Endnotes on True Stories 187

Acknowledgments 189

*To Jonathan, Vivienne, and George,
with gratitude for all the ways you remind me to be free*

Holy Trinity: An Invocation

There are at least three little girls in me.

There is the six-year-old,
newly-baptized cooking leaves over a tiny fire.
Skin as fair as cool milk freckled with brown sugar.
She is yet to be burdened by America;
she is in her primordial state,
not yet burdened by her father's anger,
her mother's dependence,
and the loss of home.

There is the seven-year-old,
now engulfed by Whiteness.
She has traded the sound of drums and Bemba songs
for stiff pews and stuffy dresses.
No one seems happy here.
America is where grandparents die, parents grieve,
and colors divide along lines that cannot be crossed.
Here her skin is fair as the European blue-eyed Jesus,

Holy Trinity: An Invocation

and there is no dancing in church.

*And then there is the one to whom I gave birth,
also from within me, and fairer still.
Hair spun from gold and eyes like the deep blue sea.
At age 3 she asks, "Mom, why is Africa important?"*

"That's where I learned how to be free."

Chapter 1

The Water & the Blood: Preliminary Thoughts

"Then you will know the truth, and the truth will set you free."
~ Jesus in John 8:32 (NIV)

"The truth will set you free, but first it will piss you off."
~ Gloria Steinem

"There is nothing about the pain of the past that I have not forgiven, but forgiveness does not mean that one forgets. It is my deep belief that in talking about the past, in understanding the things that have happened to us we can heal and go forward."
~ bell hooks in Remembered Rapture

THERE IS ONLY ONE SONG I KNOW IN BOTH ENGLISH and Chibemba. I started singing it to my daughter when she was fresh from the womb, hoping that it would calm her the way it does me.

Rock of ages, cleft for me,
let me hide myself in thee.

Amelia K. Fulbright

Let the water and the blood
from thy wounded side which flowed
be for sin a double cure.
Saves from wrath and makes me pure.

Mwe chilibwe ca kale
Kamfisame muli mwe
Umulopa na menshi
Fyansumine kuli 'mwe
E kundapwa qua fibi
Nsangululwe muntule

First the primordial waters of chaos.
Then, the blood of animal and human kinship.

First the water breaks.
Then the blood of new life breaking forth.

First the waters of Baptism.
Then the Communion body and blood

But in ChiBemba it goes the other way around. "Umulopa na menshi"---the blood and the water.

The Meal of bread & wine, body & blood.
Then the Covenant of Belonging.

The monthly cycle of menstruation.
Then the watery womb.

Suffering
then cleansing.

On the particular night in question, Vivienne had asked me to sing her to sleep. I decided on Mwe Chilibwe and began to sing, first Bemba, then English. She giggled, "Mommy, is that Spanish?"

"No, baby, it's Chibemba."

"Chibem-butt?" she giggled once more.

A few repetitions later she was fast asleep.

On the following night, the scene unfolded similarly. I sang, "Rock of Ages, cleft for me...mwe chilibwe ca kale."

"Mommy, that song worries me. Sing something happy."

It worries me, too, baby. The images of blood sacrifice and a wrathful God offend my wiser theological sensibilities. The fact that white Western theological ideas, and not our best ones, were exported to such an extent that Indigenous Zambian people now sing of them in their mother tongue---this worries me.

But it is the *only* song I know in both Chibemba and English. For me it is a bridge between my formative years spent as a missionary kid in Zambia and my white Welsh-Irish bloodline. It is the sordid sonic hybrid of my identity, partly rooted in the so-called Dark Continent, where creation itself was cradled from birth, and partly formed by rural white Appalachian and American evangelical subcultures. In this 18th century hymn and its translation are held together the American South and the global South, both of whom are my mothers.

This memoir, although roughly chronological, goes in reverse. It is the Bemba version of my life---blood then water, pain then purity. Not a revisionist history, but a hindsight attempt to see with greater clarity the ways I have been formed by both Whiteness and Africa. The ways in which the Africa in me resists becoming fully colonized or fully colonizer and the ways in which Whiteness persists in trying to conquer and control. It is about the ways I have sinned and need to repent and the ways I owe reparations for the sins of my fathers.

It is also about trial by fire and baptism in the Spirit. And the cleansing waters of rebirth. It is about looking back so I can move forward again.

Chapter 2

The Mumbi, age 6

[Flashback] The Mumbi: where I found my sacred pulse for the first time. Carving a narrow vein of lifeblood across the dry earth, the Mumbi is a clear, swift-moving stream that flows through the heart of Kalwa Farm in western Zambia. As a young child, it was my favorite swimming hole, alive with warmth and delight. But on the day of my baptism, the water was icy cold, transfused with daily showers brought on by the rainy season.

I am standing there, frozen, in my Dukes of Hazzard sweatshirt and jeans, noticing the clatter of my uncle cooking breakfast on the outdoor stove. Early morning, and light streams in over the horizon. I wade into the water with my father, who stands ready to mark me with the sign of the Trinity. Like the stone cliff that stands guard to one side of the river, my father is reliable but distant. From the other bank, my brother keeps watch. Also protective, yet more playful and within reach.

When I emerge from those frigid waters, I marvel that I actually feel different. All of six years old, and I distinctly remember thinking that baptized Christians should not bite people.

As I wipe my eyes to rescue a stray lash, salty tears send the river of my thoughts drifting backward toward a night from weeks before. I am lying in bed, frozen, while spirits ruminating on after-life dart back and forth across the shadowy Sheol of my psyche. The room is dark in the way only a Zambian night can be, and my heart drums loudly in my ear. In short: I am afraid to die and be utterly alone in hell, and the only way out that has been offered to me is Jesus.

So I swallow hard, throw off the covers, leap to the floor, and pound into the living room, where my mother lingers in her chair, quietly marinating in the last hour of generator light. I call out, "It's time!" and beseech her with a painful urgency that I'm ready to be saved. Tonight. Ever responsive, my mother walks swiftly down the hallway to summon my father. When they return, they are ecstatic but to my surprise, not startled. We bow our heads and pray together, letting the fear drain from my body and sealing my heart with a sanguine amen.

For such a transcendent occasion, that moment in the night passed quickly. But other preparations unfolded more deliberately. In the weeks that followed, I practiced the baptismal choreography with my father. I would stand in the living room, still, my two hands with palms facing upward and stacked one on top of the other. Then my father would place his right hand in the center of my back and his left hand underneath mine. Together we would gently raise our hands to my face, covering my nose and mouth---first my tiny hands, then his large one on top for greater security. A rehearsal of intimacy. I would hold my breath and close my eyes as he dipped me backward into the imaginary river. Finally he would lift me to the surface, saying something about the Father, the Son, and the Holy Ghost. It was hard to tell whether we were dancing or I was drowning, but such is the nature of the spiritual life.

In my child's mind, the waters of baptism would save me from the fires of hell. Whatever church doctrine might say, hell to me meant isolation from the people and places I loved. I knew it was time for baptism because I knew that only a few months later, our family would travel across a vast expanse of ocean to furlough in the US. I knew I needed to be immersed in The Mumbi. What I did not know at the time is that our furlough would extend permanently, and I would never say a proper goodbye to my birthplace. Not even full immersion will always keep you out of hell.

But a font, or a pool, or a river can help you survive it. These days I make my annual pilgrimage to the gulf. I swim out as far as I safely can, letting the salt cure my wounds and the waves carry me forward. I remember the Mumbi and dream: What is this sacred mystery where the waters of the earth make us clean and whole and connected again?

Chapter 3

How I Learned Racism, age 8

I was born in a small, mining town on the Copper Belt called Kalulushi, and I held dual Zambian-American citizenship until it was no longer legal to maintain both. My mother recalls that I was the only white infant in the nursery at the time of my birth, and most of the children I played with at this young age were Black Africans. I still remember my best friend, Ruth Chimfumpa. I have a vision of her in a yellow dress and a vague memory of her laughter. Despite some barriers of language, we communicated just fine, playing the kind of universal games that kids do. My mother says I used to come to her periodically, scrubbing the pale skin of my arm and insisting, "Look, Mommy, I think I'm getting darker!" I so wanted to match the people around me, as children do.

To be sure, my family enjoyed a great deal of privilege in Zambia. We were white Americans and, relative to the people around us, quite wealthy. I don't claim that there was no racism going on in that system, but I initially was shielded from it by the innocence of childhood.

My family returned to the US when I was six years old, and when I was about eight, we moved to rural North Carolina. I have a distinct memory of walking into a second grade classroom and trying to sit at a reading table with a group of African-American students. I cannot recall the dialogue precisely, but I remember that Vicky, one of my Black classmates, asked pointedly why I wanted to sit with 'them.' I didn't really understand the question, but I received the message. Up until that stage of my life, I had trusted Blackness more than whiteness. Being with Black people felt like being in my Zambian home. My mother tells how, when we first returned to the States, I would approach Black strangers in grocery stores and malls without any sense of trepidation, not understanding the legacy of "separate but equal" segregation in the South. She recalls that I hesitated more with white family than with Black strangers.

But on that particular morning at Taylorsville Elementary, I learned that in America, Blackness couldn't trust me. Even as a child, I experienced this momentary rejection with a deep sense of alienation, and that feeling has only intensified with age. As I write this memoir in my mid-forties, in a period of increasing self-awareness about how white supremacy has shaped and distorted my consciousness for four decades now, I am disturbed at how white my circle of closest friends has become. And how devoid my social circle is of Black people in particular. Not because I have thoughtfully designed it this way, but because I have not resisted my racialized consciousness thoughtfully enough to make it *another* way. To be sure, I have Black colleagues. I have many Black acquaintances. I have mentored African-American college students and pastored Black parishioners. I intentionally support Black-owned businesses. I have dated Black men. But I miss the days when my closest companion was Ruth;

the days before it ever occurred to me that our friendship across color lines was anything but natural. The days before the pores of our skin began to dry up and the layers of dermis hardened into walls, turning melanin into a mystery for me. The days before I was taught that Blackness should call forth distance and distrust, rather than connection and delight.

I eventually met Toshia, another African-American girl, and we became good friends. Oddly enough, though we were good friends, I don't ever remember going to her house to play. I invited her to my house on at least a few occasions, but I never saw where she called home. Did she not trust me enough to invite me there? Did she imagine I would not feel comfortable? Was there something about home that she did not want me to know? Or maybe there was something about *me* that she did not want home to know? Maybe home was something she wanted to keep for herself. Sometimes white folks have trouble understanding that everything is not *for* us, that we are not entitled to every territory and every place that someone else calls home.

By middle school, Toshia and I, too, had drifted apart and retreated to the corners marked "Black" and "white." I don't exactly know why; I have no memory of a fight or falling out. It just happened, as if it were the natural thing to do. As if young children could be forgiven for not grasping the logic of racial segregation, but this grace could not be extended into maturity.

That is racism in America---it is so pervasive and systemic that it feels like the natural thing to do. It is instilled in us from the beginning. And if, like me, you aren't here from the beginning, you must take a crash course. You must form a racialized consciousness to survive---socially, politically, and quite literally, if you are Black. Since that first encounter with Vicky at a reading table, I have been slowly but surely learning why her second-grade suspicion of me was well-founded.

But what a growing racialized consciousness has never stolen from me is the memory of a time when I looked at Black people and black skin without any sort of Other-ing.

I remember a time when I associated Blackness with safety.

I remember a time when I associated Blackness with generosity.

I remember a time when I associated Blackness with friendship and joy and freedom.

I imagine that this memory is not unlike what our common ancestor Eve may have experienced decades after her eviction from Eden, "I remember what it was like to be naked and not ashamed. A time when Adam and I knew nothing except a deep sense of worthiness and belonging. Before we were deceived."

Chapter 4

Shaka Zulu, age 11

"To be African American is to be African without any memory and American without any privilege."
~ James Baldwin

[Flashback] I can hear Elton calling out to me, shouting "Shaka Zulu!" as I run up the stairs and back to class after lunch. Elton was one of the boys who had teased me mercilessly in fourth and fifth grade, so when I hear him calling, "Shaka Zulu! Shaka Zulu!," it is the medicine of belonging. He is still teasing me, but in a way that says, "I see you, and I think you're okay."

∼

The year is 1989. Elton and I are in sixth grade now, and I have recently returned from Zambia---my first trip back since leaving Africa, without the chance to say goodbye, in 1984. I still own a fuschia T-shirt with the words "Africa '89" inscribed in large Black block letters on the front. At the same time, PBS is airing a mini-series about Shaka Zulu, the great warrior-king who united an African nation against impinging colonial rule. I recall being glued to the television for every episode of the Shaka Zulu mini-series; I grasped for anything and everything that would give me a sense of connection to the home that I had lost. Elton and several other Black students had been tuning in, as well. The show was a topic of conversation during the down time in class. It was not lost on me that the other white kids were not watching "Shaka Zulu," and it was not lost on Elton, either.

When my family left Zambia in 1984, my parents had intended that our sojourn back to the US be a furlough only. My older sister had just graduated from Rift Valley Academy in Kijabe, Kenya. We would spend the following year getting her settled at a small college in North Carolina, spend time with family, visit churches telling our missionary stories, and stock up on supplies before packing a large crate and returning home. That was my understanding as a 6-year-old. To hear my parents tell it, we had returned "home" from Zambia to the States and would be returning to the mission field a year later. Even within my nuclear family, we did not all share the same reference point for home.

A combination of events, the complexities of which I may never fully understand, led my parents not to return to the mission field. That is to say they never took me home. So when my mother and I had the opportunity to spend several weeks in Zambia and Kenya approximately five years after that traumatic uprooting, an opportunity for some measure of closure emerged.

The convergence of these two events---my return trip to Zambia and the airing of "Shaka Zulu"---made way for a bridging of relationships and themes. My mother and I took our trip during the school year, which meant I needed permission to miss school for an extended period. Permission was granted, provided that I report back to my fellow students on my travels. When we returned to the US, I created a presentation about the continent of Africa, with sections on geography, languages, and culture. I brought pictures and games and food, and I felt such pride in being able to educate my peers about a place none had visited and most knew little about. This sharing of knowledge and experience enabled me to begin remembering a fractured part of my identity. To own what was true, namely that "I'm not from around here," and then to point to a country across the ocean and claim it as home was healing.

This staking out of ground, however, proved problematic for my sense of place within the social geography of sixth grade: Do I belong if I am not from around here? And what is a "home"? Is it where you are born? Or where you are nurtured? Or where your worldview is formed? Or where the truth about who you are is nourished?

Taylorsville, North Carolina is a small town in the rural foothills of the Appalachian Mountains. If you are an outsider moving into the community, folks will be suspicious of you by default. It was a question from the beginning whether we ever would belong, or even whether we desired to. By sixth grade, I had made my peace with the question, though I was no closer to an answer.

These are privileged questions, of course. It is a privilege to have resources that allow one to travel across the globe with intention, to be mobile in the pursuit of a dream or a calling. It is a privilege to choose where you go, instead of being either driven out and displaced by greedy colonizers or violently shipped away from your homeland and enslaved by the same.

To call more than one place "home" and to be able to choose which home to return to—I don't take these things for granted.

In retrospect, just as my racialized consciousness began to solidify around a reading table at Taylorsville Elementary in the spring of 1986, I now perceive that my anti-racist consciousness was being formed in the same school in the fall of 1989. I started to see color in a new way, not as something purely aesthetic but as code for the weight of alienation and loss that many African-Americans carry with them daily, wondering if America really is home.

My own traumatic experience of the loss of home gave me tools for a growing empathy. What I can articulate now, I believe I knew then intuitively---namely that there was a fundamental unfairness about my connection to Africa. I could not articulate it then, and I struggle to do so now. Here is my best attempt:

> *It is wrong that a young white American girl would have an intimate, first-hand knowledge of the African continent, while her classmates, the descendants of African slaves, knew only what they could consume on TV or in other media or through the distant memories of generations gone before, or from what was told to them by this young white American girl.*

For my Black classmates, I was an unlikely bridge to their homeland. I wonder if this confounded them? I know I was attracted to my Black classmates in a way that was confounding to me. Their very bodies and their Blackness reminded me of what I loved, what I had lost, and what was never fully mine to begin with.

In a strange way I imagine that Elton and I both reminded

each other of home, not in the same way and not the same kind of home. Not the same kind of loss or grief. Mine was a devastating personal loss, but less than a decade old; his had been simmering for centuries in our collective unconscious. But it was a bond nonetheless, a visceral attachment to the continent that is the birthplace of all humanity. A vestige of a time before the lie of white supremacy.

Chapter 5

Early Signs of OCD

Around the age of seven or eight, I recall one Sunday morning walking back to our house from church, which was right next door. I am obsessively trying to smooth out the wrinkles in my dress, not wrinkles from a lack of ironing—my mother was faithful in her ironing. It was simply the natural bunching of material that occurs when one walks down a sidewalk toward home. I am distressed because it will not stay smooth. I flatten and press with my fingers and palms, repeatedly, but the results are fleeting at best. No matter what I do I cannot make it perfect. I cannot make it stay.

When I learned how to write in cursive, I had trouble finishing my school work because I agonized over the shape of every letter and curve. One year I almost missed the class Christmas party as I struggled to finish an assignment on time. That was third grade. In fourth grade, my teacher told me that my writing looked like it came off a printing press.

When I started shaving my legs, I nicked and sliced myself repeatedly, especially around the knees and ankles, searching for every single last hair. That was late elementary, early middle school.

One year I had to recopy every single shaded bubble of my scantron sheet for standardized testing. I grew up on standardized testing, and I still hear the liturgy of the test proctor resounding in my ear, "Please make your mark heavy and dark." No one ever says how heavy or how dark. That year I had become so focused on the heavy and the dark that my marks bled through to the other side of the paper, causing the entire sheet to be unreadable in the scanner. So, I had to spend hours in the guidance counselor's office re-shading every single bubble on a pristine new scantron sheet. Heavy and dark, they said, but not *too* heavy or dark. What I remember most distinctly is how clearly annoyed the guidance counselor was with me. I was in middle school.

I see now that I was searching for a modicum of control over all the chaos and loss of those early years. It was as if I truly believed that by making my letters perfectly enough, and my skin smooth enough, and my dress flat enough, the larger problems of life might be ironed out, as well.

Chapter 6

Therapy

My first instance of an actual mental health diagnosis came during my third grade year. I was having trouble eating and found myself beset by a low grade but persistent melancholy and malaise. My mother took me to our family physician—an older, gray-haired, gentle man. He wisely discerned that my condition was emotional, not physical, that I was depressed. In retrospect, I think it was a combination of things—my deep grief at not returning to Zambia, paired with my growing awareness and dismay at the way race and Whiteness were functioning in the US, ways that restricted and narrowed my potential range of experience and expression. And then there was the fact that my third grade teacher was not a particularly kind woman, and I was an especially sensitive girl. Mrs. Moffet had a penchant for making students write sentences (paragraphs, actually) for even the most minor infractions.

I don't remember us doing anything *about* the depression per se. It eventually lifted, and by fourth grade I was feeling somewhat more adjusted and content in this strange new-to-me American, Southern subculture. But it was the first time I had a name for my sadness, and that made a difference. Naming a thing can give you some power over it.

In middle school the melancholy returned. I had a debilitating fear that my friends didn't really like me, and feelings of insecurity and self-loathing overwhelmed me. This time my mother took me to see a therapist. We drove an hour each way from our rural town to Winston-Salem, where the Baptist Hospital system had a pastoral counseling department.

At each visit, my mom and I took an elevator to one of the upper floors. My mom sat in the waiting room while I joined the therapist in his office. It was a small-ish room, with soft lamp light. I recall sitting on the proverbial psychotherapy couch, which was just a boring gray couch. But the therapist himself was lovely. I had never known a man like him. I wish I could remember his name; I can't. What I do recall is *how* he was—soft-spoken and kind, yet solid. His energy invited trust, confidence, vulnerability. It was a new thing to speak so freely about my interior life with a man, and what I realize in retrospect is that he was modeling a different form of masculinity than what I had come to expect at home, and virtually everywhere else. One of the greatest gifts he gave me was the insight that my mental health struggles were a function, at least in part, by the dis-ease of my family system—not just a personal problem or a character flaw.

At a certain point, the therapist invited my parents—both mother *and* father—into a couple of family sessions. It was extraordinary that my father even agreed to attend the session (and I think there was only one he actually attended), so I took that much as a sign of his love for me and concern about my health. But when it really counted, my dad just couldn't show up. What I mean is this:

During the session that my father attended, the conversation turned at one point to how my father himself might be contributing to my distress. This, of course, is a classic technique in therapy. The therapist tries to facilitate conversations between loved ones that they may not naturally engage on their own. For me, it provided a container where I could feel safe enough to tell my truth. When I think of that day, two main memories stick. The first is that my father quickly became agitated, particularly at the therapist, but also at all of us, my mother and me included. "You're ganging up on me!" my father accused. This was pretty much always how it went at home; any attempt to reflect back to my dad how something he had said or done caused harm was met with defensiveness that quickly devolved into hostility. 'You're ganging up on me!' was a familiar refrain in our household, always sung from my father's lips. It was the chorus of a man who had deep unresolved trauma from his own childhood. My father never spoke of this, but at some point my mother explained that my dad's dad, my Grandpa Fulbright, had been physically abusive to my dad and to my grandmother. And as the oldest of four children, my dad was the one who had been burdened with both the most responsibility for chores around the farm and with the punishment for whatever my grandfather perceived had gone wrong on a given day or week. The story goes that sometime around my dad's eighteenth birthday, after his high school graduation and before he shipped off to the army, there was an altercation between my dad and my grandfather. It culminated when my dad punched his own father in the face, in an attempt to protect his mother from harm.

It is the nature of unresolved trauma that we keep living out old narratives in the context of new stories. My dad felt that constructive criticism and accountability, even from his own child, were unfair assaults. The problem was that a session designed to help my parents more effectively parent me became a session in which the therapist had to change his focus in order to re-parent my father. I remember my therapist skillfully trying to simultaneously confront, disarm, and console my dad. I worried that my mother and I would face emotional consequences at home for "ganging up" on him.

The second memory of that day that never seems to subside is that the therapist, despite my dad's very clear resistance, sent him away with homework. My dad's assignment was simple: Once a day, he was charged with telling me about a mistake he'd made that day. It could be anything as negligible as a typo or something of greater consequence, like a lost temper or a misstep at work. In therapy it had become clear that I was struggling mightily with a form of perfectionism. I lived out of a conviction that I needed to be perfect to be worthy of love and belonging. It was one of my earliest articles of faith, and one I have spent more than two decades of adulthood deconstructing. In my child's mind, I believed that if I was perfect, my dad wouldn't fly into a rage. If I was perfect, my dad wouldn't be depressed. If I was perfect, my parents would get along. I think that somewhere deep down, I even believed that if I was perfect, I would get to go home again. To the real home, the Zambian home.

This 'doctrine of perfection' harmonized well with the doctrine of original sin that I had learned about in church. This is the theological idea that all humans are born into sin, before we ever say a word or take a step, as if it were a sexually transmitted disease or a universal birth defect. As the theology goes, this is why we all need Jesus, because "all have sinned and fallen short of the glory of God" from our first breath. The logic of Christian orthodoxy is that you don't have to be perfect because Jesus the Christ was perfect, and if you believe in him, Jesus will impute his righteous perfection onto you as a kind of spiritual soul transfusion. This should have been some comfort to me. As a child I believed in Jesus with all my heart. But Jesus was, let's say, not very tangible. My father, on the other hand, was real flesh and blood, and as a minister and missionary, he was my most concrete example of what it meant to believe. And my father *believed* in perfection. Once when I was in first or second grade, my dad and I ventured out on a father-daughter date. First a game of putt-putt, followed by a trip to the theater to see the new CareBears movie. At the putt-putt course, my dad (an avid golfer) became so frustrated by my imprecise putting that he scolded, angrily instructing me on what I was doing wrong and how to fix it. "Dad, it's just putt-putt! This is supposed to be fun!" I asserted through desperate tears.

At the end of the family session, my mom, dad, and I took the elevator downstairs. It was a long, awkward, heart-heavy journey. My dad had met me there physically, but he had not met me there emotionally. And he never did his homework. Not even once. He never confessed to a single mistake.

Chapter 7

Boys Outside the Bandroom

It was like a crossroads. To the left were the bathrooms, divided for girls and boys. To the right was a short corridor leading to the bandroom. On the other side was the eighth grade hallway. At the intersection of these pale yellow cinder block walls, I waded and wobbled through puberty and into adulthood, not always knowing which way to turn or how to steady myself.

Jason: White, tall, black hair, a mustache, ninth grade.

I started going with Jason sometime during my seventh grade year of junior high. "Going together"--- that's what we called it. Unsurprisingly this often prompted the follow-up question, "Where are you going?" from parents and other grown-ups. The proper response to this, of course, is to roll your eyes in the way only teenagers can do.

My friend Molly had pretty much arranged the whole thing. Molly and I had been solid friends since elementary. We had been in an all-girl New Kids On the Block cover band that practiced in her parents' basement. We had been through the growth of armpit hair and the inaugural visits of Aunt Flow. By junior high I was well into my awkward phase, and Molly less so. She was what she has always been---thin, tan, blonde, and bubbly. She quickly transcended into one of the most popular girls in school. I became one of the "smart girls." I had friends; I was not an outcast. And Molly was not unintelligent. But junior high did not allow for that much nuance. I was smart, and she was popular.

Although we weren't as close as before, we remained friends, in large part due to Molly being popular but not stuck up. When she found out that Jason thought I was cute, she used her popularity to make the match. I was not particularly attracted to him, but I thought it would be good social credit for me to be going with a ninth grader like Jason. Something about an older man taking interest in you.

So we made it official. He gave me his yellow gold rope chain with cross pendant to wear, as a sign of our commitment. This made my mother nervous. It conveyed a level of seriousness that seemed premature to her. I thought she just didn't understand going together.

Jason would walk me to and from class. At the bell he would scurry over from the ninth grade hallway to the seventh grade one, escort me to my class, and then hurry on to his own. I had band for the final hour of each day, so Jason would take me to the crossroads between the bathrooms and the band room and say his farewell.

On the day in question, Jason and I pause in the intersection. He bends his six foot frame and plants a quick but firm kiss on my lips, getting away on foot before I can say or do anything. Like he has stolen a pack of gum from the 7-11.

I am mortified. And it's not because I feel sexually violated.

Whatever principles of consent I might apply in this situation can only apply in retrospect. I really didn't mind that he kissed me, and I didn't mind the kiss itself. I am mortified because kissing in the hallways is against the rules, and at this stage in my life, I do not break rules.

That was the end. Twenty-four hours later I had broken up with him, giving very little explanation.

Matt: White, medium height, black hair, also a mustache, eighth grade.

I suppose my crush on Matt had also begun in my seventh grade year. As I remember it, we met in AG English class. AG meaning "academically gifted."

On the day in question, Heather, Leslie, Shea, and I are standing toward the far end of the bandroom, putting away our instruments at the end of another school day. Matt and his section-mate were placing their trumpets in cases and preparing to head home.

Shea and I are having some kind of argument. Shea and I are supposed to be best friends, and we were until this day, this moment. The sequence of events has gotten jumbled in my head, all these years later. Several scenes project themselves forward in my mind, and I do not recall which happened first.

Shea is holding up a standard 8.5 X 11 inch sheet of paper. On the left hand side she has sketched a simple rendition of me, a stick figure, standing lifeless and unsuspecting. To the far right side, she has drawn a handgun. The gun hangs in mid-air, while the one wielding this weapon remains invisible. And yet someone has pulled the trigger because a line of bullets stretches in single file across the page, before finally making impact with the side of my head. Shea laughs. I am not amused.

We argue, about what I'm not sure, and at some point, my

retort sends her into a posture of retaliation. She yells across the bandroom, "Matt, you know Amelia has a crush on you, right?!" Laughter, spiteful laughter, echoes in my ear. It is the meanest thing anyone has ever done to me. Matt being Matt, looks up, acknowledging that he has heard, and then walks quietly out the bandroom door.

I am awkward, nauseated, and mortified, like Shea's two-dimensional sketch on that page. Finding nowhere to hide and feeling hot tears well up inside, I grab my things and hurry out the door. At the crossroads I look both ways, before finally taking refuge in the bathroom.

End scene. End friendship.

I don't remember ever cutting off a relationship the way I cut Shea out of my life. For about a year, almost all of eighth grade, we did not speak. We did not sit together at lunch, or exercise together in P.E., or room together on class trips. I gravitated toward a new group of friends.

There was a name for my new girlfriends, a name which I will not repeat because it contains an awful racist slur. They tended to date Black boys, like Elton. They were exploring their sexuality in ways that Heather, Leslie, Shea, and I had not yet imagined. This new group of friends posed some risks for me in terms of reputation, which is to say that I was a "good" girl, and by entirely racist and patriarchal definitions, they were not.

Occasionally I found myself in situations that made me uneasy, like when we had boys in our hotel room past curfew one night during our class trip to Washington, DC. But I loved these new friends. They were true friends, not mean girls like Shea, and they healed my heart. And the truth is that they were not "exploring their sexuality" anymore than other white girls were with white boys. The truth is that they were stigmatized because Black sexuality is stigmatized. Pubescent white boys get to be boys, Whiteness says, and pubescent Black boys are dangerous, especially to young white women.

Monty: African-American, medium height, ninth grade.

On the day in question, I make my way out of the bandroom, down the short corridor and into the crossroads once again.

Monty seems to come out of nowhere. He grabs my right forearm and pulls me in close.

"Go out with me," he says, not as a question, more like a demand.

"I'm not interested, " I say gently, pushing down fear.

"Why not?" he says, "is it because I'm Black?"

"No, I'm just not interested."

He holds on for what is probably seconds, but feels like minutes. Finally, he releases his grip and moves on. "I'll call you later," he says, glancing back before turning the corner.

And he did call; he called several more times before he took no for an answer. I do not know if he really liked me or if he saw me as a kind of prize. This was a conflict in our middle school. Black boys wanting to date white girls on account of their whiteness, which justifiably angered Black girls. Around the same time, a seventh grader had brought a handgun to school inside her backpack. Apparently she was involved in a dispute with another student, a Black girl, over a Black boy they both were interested in. Fortunately no shots were fired, and no one was physically hurt. Later that year metal detectors were installed at all entrances, and a young white police officer was assigned to regular duty at our school. I did not want to be caught up in the middle of this struggle.

But the deeper truth is that I felt threatened because of the way he held on to me. The ugly truth is that I felt more threatened because he was Black. Floating around in my subconscious were ideas about how Black men are more sexually aggressive, mature faster, and are likely to make unwanted advances toward white women. You can trace these racist ideas all the way back to Emmett Till, who lost his life because a white woman felt uncomfortable about the way he looked at her.

In that moment Whiteness also prevented me from ever considering that Monty may have actually liked me, for me. While not life-threatening, that distortion was not benign. Maybe there was something valid about his desire? Some wisdom or delight on his part that could have been a gift to me, even if I could not reciprocate the attraction...my loss, perhaps, more than his.

End scene.

Chapter 8

Testing the Bonds

The summer before my senior year of high school, my family loaded up a moving truck and relocated to Greenville, North Carolina, a university town in the eastern part of the state, only a couple hours from the beach. The home of East Carolina University and its associated medical school, Greenville, attracted a more diverse and growing population than the rural community we were leaving, and it was situated in a region of North Carolina with a more progressive social and political history. By the time we left Taylorsville, I had made some really solid friends, and I most assuredly grieved leaving them. But mostly I was excited about this new adventure, particularly because the city of Greenville held the promise of a more open, expansive, inclusive community.

But in the meantime, I had been accepted to attend the North Carolina School of Science and Mathematics, a magnet school that attracted high school juniors and seniors from across the state to study in advanced classes, some of which were taught by professors who also held positions in one of the nearby universities. My US History professor, for instance, also taught at Duke. NCSSM required students to live at their residential campus in Durham, which meant that in the summer, I moved to Greenville, and in the fall I moved to Durham.

My classmates at NCSSM were some of the most wonderfully weird people I'd ever met. All nerds, by definition, but also artists, and queers (though we didn't use that word back then), and the variously quirky. Pretty much everyone who came to the school had some experience of not quite fitting in at the high school back home. There was the kid who'd gotten a perfect 1600 score on his SAT, when he was barely out of middle school. The theater kids and Tori Amos devotees whose creative imaginations simply got stifled in more traditional school settings. Or kids like me, third culture kids with a global consciousness, who felt most at home being one weirdo among many.

But it was also weird going through multiple moves in a few months' time. I didn't quite know where I belonged... again. I also had this realization that starting at a residential high school my junior year meant that I essentially had moved out and gone to college two years early. When I started to consider leaving NCSSM and finishing out my high school years in Greenville, my older sister thought I was reckless to pass up such a prestigious opportunity. I understood where she was coming from. She had attended boarding school in Kenya, an entirely different country, during her high school years when my family lived in Zambia. But I just wasn't ready for that more permanent break from home. And I was depressed again, not eating enough, losing weight, and struggling to reach out for connection. I determined to finish out the fall semester of my junior year in Durham and then to move back to Greenville to live with my parents and finish high school.

Healthy relational attachment is a strange thing. When we are newborns, bonding with our parents or primary caregivers is essential for us to thrive. A secure bond in infancy can lay the foundation for a lifetime of stable relationships, while the absence of that bond can leave us on shaky ground as we mature. When we become toddlers and begin to test the boundaries of our independence, we experiment with greater and greater periods of distance and separation from our grownups, but we keep coming back to check in and to make sure that the foundational bond is still secure. Paradoxically, the more secure our primary bonds, the more likely we are to feel safe and empowered to venture out further and further into the whole, wide world. I had really tried to venture out and make a new life in Durham, but I needed to run back home to see if the bonds would still hold.

Chapter 9

Who Would Jesus Divorce?

During the early '90s, everyone was asking "What Would Jesus Do?" WWJD, for short, popped up on bracelets and hoodies—a clever and fairly superficial rebranding of the Social Gospel movement that originally had emerged in the late 1800s in response to Charles Sheldon's book *In His Steps: What Would Jesus Do*. The novel *In His Steps*, which I read sometime in the '90s myself, had to do with a pastor and a Christian community that was transformed by turning their attention to caring for the poor. You know, like Jesus did. When the early twentieth century theologian Walter Rauschenbusch articulated his vision of the Social Gospel, which was a form of Christian Socialism, he cited Sheldon's novel as inspiration. But the WWJD slogan of the 1990s felt more like the tagline for a social club than a spiritual or social justice movement.

In my circles, WWJD got mingled with a form of pious American Evangelicalism that was obsessed with right belief and sexual purity and individual sins, rather than collective social evils like corporate greed, the military-industrial complex, and systemic oppression. It was more socializing than socialism. What Would Jesus Do? Not have premarital sex. What Would Jesus Do? Listen to contemporary Christian music. What Would Jesus Do? Avoid the gays and the heathens.

In hindsight my view of the WWJD movement is quite jaded, as you can tell, but even at the time I felt a certain uneasiness about it. What could have been a freedom cry had been converted into a tool for indoctrination.

To be fair, when my mother handed me a copy of *In His Steps*, her motivation was genuine. One of the novel's main characters is a homeless man who challenges the local pastor to take seriously Jesus' example of caring for the most marginalized community members. I imagine that my mom saw her brother in these pages. My uncle Jimbo had lived on the streets of Raleigh, North Carolina for many years, and during the '90s I made many trips downtown with my mom to find and check in on Jimbo. We brought him clean clothes, especially socks, took him to lunch, and occasionally even brought him back to our house for dinner. My mother indeed was living out her own personal social Gospel.

The bottom line, though, is that in the '90s, no one ever suggested to me that Jesus would challenge the very structures and hierarchies and systems that keep people poor and bound in the first place, though this is in fact what Jesus of the Gospels did. He not only addressed poverty and disease, he challenged the policies and politics that kept them in place, and he did so in families, in faith communities, and in the face of empire.

∽

When I sat in the car with my mother that day, probably in 1995 or 1996, I should have known that she ultimately would ask, "What Would Jesus Do?" But in that moment, she wasn't asking Jesus; she was asking me.

"How would you feel if I divorced Dad?" This was a topic of discussion that had come up a few times before. Things had not been good at home for as long as I could remember. The only time I recall my parents' marriage being healthy and my father not being prone to outbursts of rage was the time before we returned to the US. But the truth is that I really have no memories of my parents' marriage prior to that time.

I believe I was a senior in high school the year we had this conversation, sitting in the car that was parked in our driveway in Greenville, North Carolina. When she asked me this question, I felt a wave of relief rise and fall through my chest. Then, the tiniest ember of hope flickered in my heart space. I let my imagination wander for a bit. I had trouble envisioning anything concrete about what our lives might be after a divorce, but I could feel it. No more walking on eggshells. No more hiding my truest thoughts and feelings. No more unpredictable eruptions of anger from my father. No more of his paranoia. No more of his constant criticism. No more feeling small and worthless inside my own house. No more keeping silent. No more lies. No more pretending to be a perfect family. No. More.

I wanted to beg her to leave, but I didn't. Carefully and calmly, I offered instead, "Mom, if you wanted to get a divorce, I would be okay with that."

My mother and I had a pact. Living together in a house with my emotionally abusive father had forged a trauma bond between us. Because he was a preacher and our whole lives centered around the protection of his reputation, we couldn't tell anyone. I mean no one. A few times I shared the bare bones of it with a friend, but otherwise our story was so shrouded in shame that we dare not utter it. Once in youth group, our ministers gently invited us to vent about any challenges we were having with our parents. I started to speak up with what I thought was a reasonably benign frustration, and one of the leaders cut me off, "What could you possibly have to complain about? Your parents are perfect!"

Because my mother had no one to confide in and because my father did not support her seeing a therapist, she relied on me as her counselor, confidant, friend. This began when I was in grade school, and I became quite practiced at parenting her. I had learned to set aside my own needs and feelings to hold space for her, to see her as a person aside from her role as my mother.

That day in the car I was talking to Ruby. I set aside for a moment that we were talking about my father, my fate. It was her marriage, her choice, her agency on the line. I gave her permission to choose. In retrospect I marvel at how my 17 or 18-year-old self could maintain such a disinterested stance about the matter, but the truth is that I was afraid to ask for what I needed. I needed my mother to draw a line in the sand and say this kind of life is unacceptable. I needed her to protect our emotional and spiritual wellbeing over some skewed sense of righteousness or propriety. I needed my mother to leave, but I was afraid to say so because I did not have confidence that she would. It felt safer not to risk that kind of disappointment at all.

There were many factors in my mom's decision not to leave. She worried that she wouldn't be able to support herself. She worried that she would ruin my dad's ministry. She worried that she would be looked down on as a divorced person, ruining her own opportunities for ministry. She also expressed fear that my older brother and sister, both of whom were out of the house at this point, would abandon her and keep her from seeing her grandchildren. This last anxiety I never quite understood. Whatever anger or unhappiness my siblings might have felt, I could not fathom them cutting off relationship with our mother. We all loved her dearly.

Her fears about losing her standing and leadership roles in Southern Baptist life may have been more realistic; it was the mid-'90s after all. But I wonder if those, too, were rooted mostly in my mother's struggle to see herself as worthy of love and belonging. This is what happens over time to people who are abused in relationships, be it physically, emotionally, spiritually, or sexually. We see ourselves as deserving of mistreatment and rejection. Or perhaps we simply lose our ability to imagine what it is to be loved well. Years later, when I worked the phones at the National Domestic Violence Hotline, I would finally have a framework to make sense of this.

A few weeks after my mom explained that she had decided not to pursue a divorce, I received a small card in the mail from a member of our church. It was from Sylvia, a good friend of my mother's and considered by many to be one of the wisest members of our congregation. Apparently my mother had broken our vow of silence in order to share some of her dilemma with Sylvia. That much was a breakthrough.

I opened the card to find a note handwritten in cursive black felt pen. It read approximately as follows, "Amelia, I hope you can understand your mom's decision not to leave. She is trying to do what Jesus would do—love your father unconditionally even when it involves sacrifice. Love, Sylvia"

Bullshit.

I felt hot with anger and utterly betrayed. At this point in my life I did not have enough training in bible or theology or feminism to properly deconstruct this argument, but in my heartspace, I very clearly understood that this had nothing to do with Jesus and everything to do with patriarchy and a terribly distorted interpretation of Christ's sacrifice on the cross. Jesus was not in an abusive relationship. He was executed by authorities who represented an unholy alliance between the religious establishment and the Roman empire. On the third day, he rose from the grave to show them that their death-dealing system would not triumph ultimately over the power of Love. More precisely, Jesus' Easter resurrection is a sign to us that God desires us to have life and to have it abundantly, not to forever be caught in cycles of unresolved trauma and abuse. Telling women to stay in abusive relationships is *not* what Jesus would do. And this is true even when there are no visible scars as evidence of the damage. Staying in this kind of relationship shows up in side effects like mental health diagnoses, chronic illness, stunted dreams, relational dysfunction, career dissatisfaction, spiritual disillusionment, and a general failure to thrive. And what's more, it does not redeem the one who abuses; they, too, are trapped inside the tomb of their own despair.

I never trusted Sylvia very much after that. Worse still, I felt that my mother had chosen everyone and everything but me—my father's reputation, her job prospects, my brother and sister's feelings, and Jesus, but not me. I had tried to offer her a way out, *us* a way out, and she didn't take it.

I, of course, will never know all the circumstances, thought exercises, or convictions that led my mother to stay when it was my deepest desire to go. What I know is that my mother never taught me how to decide when it's time to leave, or that leaving and letting go can be part of the healing and holy repertoire for human flourishing. I suppose no one ever taught her, either. For my mother, it has always been about staying, never going. Laboring endlessly to create a facsimile of wholeness, if not the total fact, which sometimes means engaging in denial and asking others to go there with you, so that the facade of family unity never cracks.

So I did what I always did. I stuffed the pain deeper down inside. I braced myself. I kept my mouth shut. I loved my momma dearly. And I held my breath until that bright August day in the late summer of 1996, when I moved into the second floor of Collins Dormitory at Wake Forest University. College is where I came up gasping for air.

Chapter 10

Hacky Sack Boys

I OFTEN STAYED UP LATE, SOMETIMES ALL NIGHT, during my freshman year of college. Everything was so new and different, exotic even, and the fear of missing out kept me from going to bed. The Hacky Sack Boys, as my older sister used to call them, were my frequent late-night companions. Long-haired, pot-smoking, jam band-seeking, journal-toting, poetry-quoting iconoclasts of the very best kind—they taught me a lot. They introduced me to the mysticism of Meister Eckhart and the music of Leonard Cohen. Most of all they taught me that the world could legitimately be seen from an entirely different vantage point than what I knew.

[Flashback] On this particular night, I am sitting around a table in one of my dorm's co-ed lounges. It is me, Jeff, Mike, another guy named Mike, and maybe someone else, I can't recall. At some point the conversation turns to religion. I can't remember why or how it takes this turn, but I clearly recall being the only one at the table who identifies as a very religious person. One of the Mikes, who was Jewish but not very

devout, sits directly across from me. It is, by all accounts, a friendly conversation.

Finally Mike leans forward across the table, looking me firmly in the eye, "So, Amelia, do you think *I'M* going to hell?" Mike understands that many Christians believe only Christians go to heaven, and that even Jews, God's chosen people, will be cast into hell if they don't "believe in Jesus." He says it playfully, half-joking, like what he can't believe is that I would believe this.

Nobody has ever asked me this question directly. I realize that, if I am going to be honest with Mike, I have to say "Yes. According to the theology I was taught growing up, I would have to say yes."

And the reality of Mike's question and my honest answer feels like too much to bear in the moment. I feel nauseous and flushed, ashamed really, so I excuse myself from the table, walk quietly back to my room, and cry silently in the dark until I fall asleep.

∼

Nobody had ever asked me this question before, and because nobody had ever asked, I had never seriously thought about the answer. I had never really stopped to consider the far-reaching and terrifying implications of my beliefs about heaven and hell, and precisely who goes where. From that point forward, I realized that I would need to either (a) reconsider my personal theology, or (b) work a whole lot harder to keep the people I knew and loved, like Mike, out of eternal damnation. That is a lot of pressure, choice (b).

The conversation with Mike changed everything. I majored in Religion, studying the major world religions and a variety of philosophies. I spent a lot more time talking to Mike, and

Mike, and Jeff. I decided to question everything *and* to study my own Christian tradition more carefully. I also worried that I might go to hell for asking too many questions, as if God were some authoritarian dictator in the sky who persecutes a free press.

I remember a second night, this time during sophomore year, again lying in my dorm room bed, wondering if I was lost, like in the evangelical sense---does not know Jesus, alienated from God, doomed, isolated, damned. Just for asking the hard questions.

The epiphany that came to me was that any God big and powerful and loving enough, any God worth believing in, could not possibly be threatened by my honest, sincere searching. Maybe that kind of God would even love me for it.

Chapter 11

The Wreck

Riding in the car with my father is a kind of captivity. He fidgets while he drives, picking at rough patches on his arms or rubbing his thumb incessantly back and forth on the opposite hand in a rote pattern I can't seem to ignore. As a child, I always wondered why I couldn't look away from these seemingly innocuous habits; I would fixate on them as if they were signs of flawed character. Now I recognize them as a form of Obsessive Compulsive Disorder, mannerisms of disease, and the experts say that OCD is often the result of childhood trauma.

Riding in the car with my father is a kind of captivity because you never know which version of him is in the driver's seat. Will it be the kindly guard who sneaks you extra morsels of food, or the one who rebukes you mercilessly, or the one who flies into a fit of rage? If he misses a traffic signal or barely misses another driver, and you flinch or holler because you were momentarily afraid, he will yell at you for not trusting him. He can't manage his own emotions, much less yours.

I finally have a rule that I won't ride with him, but when I was in my early twenties, an accident forced me to ride in the car with my father. I can't remember if it was Christmas or summer break, junior or senior year of college. I do remember that my head was so full and my heart so numb that I couldn't be present in my body. Distracted at the level of soul, I crashed my car into a cement light post in a parking lot.

It was around the same time I started taking Prozac. That was when the dreams started, too. They alternated between psychedelic visions of dancing elephants, stolen from Disney's *Fantasia*, and vivid scenes of me yelling at my father---long, angry tirades that had been building since I was small. Often the tirades would end only because I startled myself awake.

It might have been the same year I went coed skinny dipping at the Baptist Student Ministry retreat. Or maybe it was senior year, when I released my virginity to my pot-smoking boyfriend. Those were some of the best times of my life—tasting the pleasure of strong drink in the throat, Parliament Funkadelic in the hips, and a lover's touch in the small of the back. But I was also a wreck, finally feeling the sting of at least a decade's worth of unresolved anger and depression. I was the prodigal daughter sowing wild oats, and my dad was *not* a metaphor for God-the-Father.

∽

So, I can't remember exactly when I collided with the light post, but that's when I found myself riding in the car with my father. His was a pick-up truck. Toyota. In my recollection, I am sure I hear country music on the radio. Probably a song about cheatin', or drinkin', or hot redneck girls---which is cliche, I know. I never understood why my father had a tolerance for this kind of moral flexibility in country songs but much less so for the hard livin' in rock'n'roll.

[Flashback] The truck is immaculate. Uncluttered and wiped clean. I catch a whiff of his Old Spice cologne and notice the hardness of his hands.

I am so afraid. I sit with a tightness, forgetting to breathe, and anticipate what will come: Will there be disbelief that I could be so careless? The heaping of guilt over costly repairs to my Camry? General disapproval? Shame disguised as parenting? I don't realize at the time that my father thinks criticism is a love language. And he never understands an unforced error.

For a while we drive in silence, heavy. Finally, he says something like this, "I get distracted a lot when I'm driving. Half the time, I know the radio's on, but I never really hear the words to the songs. I know you have a lot on your mind. Next time you'll know to pay more attention."

No wounding words. No air of condemnation. All Grace. And even a moment of recognition.

Now and then going home surprises you. The prodigal returns, and the father is redeemed.

Chapter 12

Divine Child Abuse

[Self-reflection] It has taken me a long time to recognize that my experience of white evangelicalism, which is in itself a product of Whiteness, was also twisted up with family trauma, generations of untreated mental illness, and emotional abuse from my father. Until I began to deconstruct the faith of my childhood, I'd had no experience of Christianity that wasn't also tied up with trauma.

Perhaps that is why Rita Nakashima Brock's description of substitutionary atonement as "divine child abuse" resonated so deeply.

I don't remember how I got there. But I remember sitting in one of the very last rows of an auditorium on the Wake Forest campus. It was probably my good friend Reagan who had invited me. We had both grown up in Baptist churches in North Carolina, although his must have been way more progressive than mine. It was Reagan who convinced me to take a Feminist Interpretations of the Bible class with Phyllis

Tribble—a truly groundbreaking feminist Hebrew Bible scholar, and I'm pretty sure he had brought me to this lecture hall, as well. I had never heard of Phyllis Trible or Rita Brock before Reagan. (As a side note: I am now Facebook friends with Rita Brock, where I get to see photos of her cats and what she ate for dinner, and have heard her speak on multiple occasions.)

Prior to this night, I also didn't know, as in *perceive*, that what I understood at the time to be THE core doctrine of Christian faith—substitutionary atonement—was such a horror. The logic of substitutionary atonement is that God (The Father) sacrifices his one and only perfect son (Jesus) in order to save the rest of God's children (us) from eternal damnation. You might recall a similar story from the Hebrew Bible, in which Abraham believes that God is calling him to sacrifice his son Isaac, but in this story God ultimately stays Abraham's hand, in a pointed critique of the child sacrifice practiced by other ancient Near Eastern cultures. But not in the version of Christian theology that is built around God the Father's sacrifice of his very own son! And somehow they make it sound like Good News, namely by telling you that you are a hopeless sinner destined to spend eternity in conscious torment, were it not for Jesus dying on a cross. If you believe that you are without hope, and the only remedy is violence—sacrifice even—I suppose you'll take your chances, even if the theology itself is so toxic that it ends up killing your soul in the process.

When Rita Nakashima called substitutionary atonement "divine child abuse," she said the quiet part out loud, she broke the silence, she told the family secret out loud, in public. I was stunned, both by her boldness and the plain truth of what she was saying. What she was saying was true, though the average Evangelical Christian does not consciously conceive of their theological framework as abusive. But we see the myth of redemptive violence plastered all over our public consciousness in American culture, whether one is Christian or not.

The wife must sacrifice for her husband.
The mother must sacrifice for her child.
The soldier must sacrifice for his country.
Even unto death,
even unto death.

This is the theology that keeps people in abusive relationships and slaves in bondage and citizens in service to the machinations of Empire and women subjugated by men. This is the theology that, at least according to Sylvia, kept my mother from divorcing my father.

Substitutionary atonement is a theology *about* Jesus, but it does not seem to be the theology *of* Jesus. In the New Testament, salvation is not escape from a literal hell; it is healing and wholeness and liberation. These are not variations on a theme; they are different themes! In substitutionary atonement thinking, someone always has to die to keep the peace, if not literally, then emotionally and spiritually. This is how we did it in my family of origin; this is still how we do it in my family of origin. We all make ourselves smaller and more palatable to him, so that my father can be appeased. Because he struggles to emotionally regulate himself, we do it for him by being just what he needs us to be. We extinguish our truth to keep him from bursting into angry flames. And we don't really talk about it, except tangentially in side conversations and quiet corners. It is our unwritten social contract, to never speak plainly about the terrible truth of things. It makes me cringe to speak about it after all these years of keeping up the facade. For all these years, we have been sacrificing ourselves to save my father, to help him save face, to protect him from ever having to encounter the truth about his own condition. The core family doctrine is not healing or wholeness or liberation; it is appeasing the Father, whose dimensions have become god-like for us. And we are not saved.

Chapter 13

Observing Silence

[Self-reflection]
I can't help you by staying small and quiet.
The only way I can help you is by getting loud and free,
and you are going to hate me for it at first.

"Were you silent or were you silenced?"
~ Oprah Winfrey,
via author Cole Arthur Riley in her book This Here Flesh

"Not everything that is faced can be changed, but nothing can be changed until it is faced."
~ James Baldwin

THE PRACTICE OF KEEPING SILENCE HAS LONG BEEN central to contemplative forms of spirituality, across religious traditions. Christian monastic orders like the Trappist monks keep silence for most of their days, punctuating the quiet with periods of chanting in worship or reading aloud. Silent mindfulness meditation, which is rooted in Zen Buddhism, can take many forms—with the goal of each being to quiet both the voice and the busy mind. When I lead worship services in my own congregation, I incorporate designated times for silent prayer. There is always a judgment to be made about how long to extend the silence. Some of those gathered will, no doubt, bask in the silence and be tempted to wander off mentally, never to return their full attention to the liturgy. I am one of those! So I remind myself to be conscious of those for whom the silence feels awkward, uncomfortable, or even unsafe. I remind the worshippers that what we are listening for in the silence is the movement of God's loving Spirit among us—the Spirit that may convict, challenge, or guide us along new pathways, but never without our consent and never without our liberation at heart.

I learned a lot about observing silence as a child. I learned the unspoken but enforced rules about which subjects were off limits and whose ideas and opinions were allowed to take up space. I learned that speaking up for oneself was almost always construed by my father as talking back. Back then I learned to survive by being small and still and, mostly, silent.

In my family of origin, the most dangerous transgression was to tell *the truth about the way things are*. I learned very early on that it was not okay to say the truth about things out loud... because the grownups couldn't handle it. Perhaps that's why telling the truth has become my deepest and most radical spiritual practice. In spite of my own affinity for sitting quietly and still, in spite of my resistance to making a scene, I have become Amelia ~ Breaker of silences; Breaker of cycles ~ both in my family and in my profession.

I have lived into this vocation slowly, reluctantly over time. When you are a breaker of silences and cycles, no one thanks you for it at first. They say all manner of things about you—

That you think you are better than them.

That you think you are smarter than them.

That you have abandoned and betrayed your family.

But the truth is that I have become a breaker of silences because the secret keeping was killing my soul. Whereas the silence once kept me safe, I am learning now to speak up and out, also as a matter of survival.

When I got a tattoo during the summer after my sophomore year of college, while doing an internship in San Francisco, my mother suggested that I not tell my father. It seemed like the wise thing to do at the time. We kept quiet about a lot of things to avoid my father's temper. It didn't take a whole lot of effort in this case because my tattoo is situated on my lower back and was rarely visible. My mother called it a "permanent painting," which I found quite poetic, and yet it also kept the truth of the thing somewhat at a distance, at arm's length enough to be palatable. My daughter doesn't have a tattoo; she has a "permanent painting."

I kept the secret for approximately two more years, until the night before my college graduation. *The truth about the way things are* welled up so full and deep inside of me. As I sat on the bed in my senior year apartment, I also sat on the verge of real adulthood, with plans to move to Cincinnati after graduation, to find a job, and my own place. In my own estimation, there was an incompatibility between being an adult and being unable to say *the truth about the way things are.*

Late that night, probably close to 10pm, I drove to my parents' hotel room, sat next to my father on the bedspread of a Super 8 Motel, and through hot tears and heavy sighs, I told the truth—that I had a tattoo and that I occasionally drank alcohol. It almost sounds comical in retrospect, but it took great courage to say those things under the enormous weight of existential dread that had kept them hidden for so long. To my father's credit, he mostly responded with compassion. He mumbled about the wastefulness of "spending good money" on something as frivolous as a "permanent painting," and he worried about my decision to drink, even socially. At the same time, something in him honored the part of me that drove me to drive myself (literally) the necessary miles to tell *the truth about the way things are*.

But the familial pattern of silence and secret keeping has persisted. Just in the last five years, well into my adulthood, there has been an unspoken expectation that I will keep quiet about the aspects of who I am that might provoke discomfort or cause an argument at the holiday dinner table—and believe me, there are A LOT of things to keep quiet about: How much of my ministry has been devoted to queer kids. My pro-choice, pro-abortion activism. My rejection of some of the basic teachings of white Evangelicalism. Voting for democrats. All of these things are off limits. Which means that the only version of myself that is truly welcome in my family of origin is so heavily edited that she virtually ceases to be me.

On a visit back to North Carolina before the pandemic, I carried a copy of The Houston Chronicle to share with my mother. The paper had recently published an Op-ed of mine, in which I outlined a pro-choice faith perspective on one of the many abortion restriction bills passing through the Texas Legislature. I was proud to be published and thought my mother would be proud of me, too. I think she *was* proud, but when I handed her the piece, she quickly shoved it under a stack of other books and papers on her dresser, so that it would be carefully hidden and out of sight. As an isolated incident, it may seem unremarkable, but it is one of many slights and signals over four decades of my life, and they have accumulated like a stack of dusty past due bills that need somehow to be reconciled and resolved.

I finally came out as queer/bisexual in June of 2022,

though I had been wrestling with this aspect of my identity for over 20 years. I distinctly remember telling myself, in my early-mid twenties, that my family could handle me being an ally but not me actually being queer. So I fearfully calibrated what was possible for me to accommodate *their* limitations, not mine. This is how silencing works. It limits and binds our hearts and minds with steady, consistent messaging that who we are, and what we know, and *the way things are* is just too much for a heart and mind, or a family, to hold. Silencing keeps us small with its insistence that the truth is just too dangerous, and so even when any imminent threat to our wellbeing is gone, the silence still lives on.

~

There is a children's volume called *The Quiet Book*, and it was given to my oldest child by my mother when Vivienne was a toddler. The book gently and cleverly illuminates all the different kinds of quiet that a child might need to navigate from day to day:

First one awake quiet.
Top of the roller coaster quiet.
First look at my new haircut quiet...

You get the picture. There are many kinds of quiet, and for kids and grownups alike, there also are many kinds of silence.

The silent awe of beholding a rose gold sunset.
The breathtaking silence of a romantic first kiss.
Receiving bad news at the doctor's office silence.
Rejection letter silence.
Crying yourself to sleep at night silence.

Hiding in the closet silence; also the silent stares when you come out.
The silence of not speaking your truth.
The silence of those who will not come to your defense.
The silence of those who will reject you for who you are.
And there also is that still, small voice of Love...in the silence.

    We must learn to ask ourselves, "Which kind of silence is this? The kind that will suffocate or the kind that will liberate?"

Chapter 14

This Flood

*When you pass through the waters, I will be with you;
and through the rivers, they shall not overwhelm you;
when you walk through fire you shall not be burned,
and the flame shall not consume you. (Isaiah 43:2)*

(Song lyrics written sometime during my senior year of college, Wake Forest University, 1999-2000.)

*I am drowning in a sea of self-awareness,
self-importance,
or the absence of both.
I see my spirit sacrificed on an altar to a god much less divine than me.
And there is blood on my hands,
And no matter how many tears I shed to resurrect this spirit slain,
my will is dead, my will is dead.*

And you are everything good that died inside me.

You're the honesty, the faith, and the hope in me.
And you are every ounce of courage and strength in my blood,
the blood that poured from my body
and washed away in this flood.
Why won't you let me be ugly, and angry, and beaten?
Let my ruin begin...

"Cause I just wanna let the water wash over me, let the darkness swallow me.
I just wanna let the brilliant flames consume me, let the fire set me free.
Why won't you let me drown in this flood?
Just let me drown in this flood.

I want to hate you, defile you, push you so far away.
Until you hate me, too.
...

Because you are everything good that died inside me.
You're the honesty, the faith, and the hope in me.
And you are every ounce of courage and strength in my blood,
the blood that poured from my body
and washed away in this flood.
Why won't you let me be ugly, and angry, and beaten?
Let my ruin begin...

"Cause I just wanna let the water wash over me, let the darkness swallow me.
I just wanna let the brilliant flames consume me, let the fire set me free.
But you won't let me drown in this flood.
You won't let me drown in this flood.

Chapter 15

Queen City Mental Health

I stood as tall as I possibly could and pulled the most authoritative voice I could find from the depths of my abdomen, "Ed, you're going to the hospital. Either you can get in my car right now, or I'll call the police and have them take you instead."

Ed, whose six foot frame towered over me, gulped loudly and eked out a sheepish, "OK."

While he was still holding on to this moment of lucidity, I led Ed out to my silver Toyota Camry and drove him directly to Psychiatric Emergency Services at the main hospital. Ed eventually was admitted to the hospital on a mental health hold and stayed for a few days, until his mental status had improved and he was stabilized on medications. I visited him in the hospital, and when he was feeling more like himself, we bonded over our shared love of country-bluegrass musician Kathy Mattea. When he was not well, Ed held a delusion that he was being followed by the legendary mobster Al Capone, accompanied by the paranoia one would expect to go along with being tracked by a gangster. When he wasn't well and off his schizophrenia meds,

Ed (a middle aged man old enough to be my dad) had trouble feeding and clothing himself and keeping his apartment in livable condition. As his case manager, it had become my job to help Ed meet his basic needs, maintain his mental health, and enjoy a quality life. Indeed, the first time I ever met Ed, my supervisor had invited me on a home visit to check in on him at his apartment. We found a dirty, cluttered, rat-infested one bedroom just north of Cincinnati's Over-the-Rhine district, and we began the process of building enough trust with Ed to help him back on the road to mental wellness and stability. Ed and I had come a long way together.

I moved to Cincinnati in the summer of 2000, after graduation from Wake Forest. My college boyfriend had grown up in one of the townships that constituted the Cincy suburbs. He was heading back there after graduation, and we decided to make the move together. My original plan was to start seminary at the Pacific School of Religion in Berkeley, California. I had been accepted and even offered a generous grant to fund tuition and living expenses. But I needed a break from school, especially after the mental health crisis I'd endured during the fall semester of my senior year. Prozac, the anti-depressant I'd been using was effective, but I still felt like I was feeling my way in the dark toward the ideal of mental health. I wasn't quite ready for a West Coast adventure.

With a degree in world religions and not much work experience outside of mission and social work contexts, I landed a job at Queen City/Mitchell Mental Health Services, i.e. QCM, Inc. As a case manager, I was responsible for managing the treatment plans of adults with a range of severe mental health diagnoses—schizophrenia, bipolar I disorder, major depression, obsessive-compulsive disorder, borderline personality disorder, trichotillomania, and more. These clients were folks who had minimal to no support from family or friends, or whose friends and family simply didn't have the capacity or skillset to sufficiently care for their loved ones. Although QCM benefited from a combination of public and private financial support, we were like most social service agencies—short-staffed and underfunded. Each of the case managers on my team regularly carried a caseload of approximately 70 or 80 clients, maybe even in the 90s if we were down a team member. That's a lot of clients, way beyond what could actually be managed.

Some of my clients lived in their own apartments, bought their own groceries, and just needed an occasional visit or ride to a medical appointment. Others cycled on and off medications, in and out of the hospital, and back and forth in their progress. Some would always need extra care, like Gloria, a short, round jolly woman who lived in a group home for adults with various disabilities. She liked to smoke a little weed every now and then. It wasn't really part of her treatment plan, but I suppose it increased her quality of life from time to time.

James, on the other hand, couldn't afford to get high. Marijuana just exacerbated his paranoia, landing him in all sorts of precarious situations. One day I picked him up at the halfway house where he lived, and he had carved swastikas into the knees of jeans. He readily confessed to having smoked a joint and then feeling inspired to decorate his pant legs. This was a really bad choice for James, a young white man in his 20s who lived in a halfway house with quite a few Black men. That day being a case manager meant explaining to James why paying homage to the Nazi regime on his Levis was a really bad idea, for the obvious reason that it is racist and the only slightly less obvious risk that it may provoke his housemates, who let's face it, James, "you don't stand a chance against in a fist fight."

Being new to Cincinnati and with a much less developed sociopolitical consciousness than I have now, I was ignorant about the long history of tense and sometimes volatile race relations in the city. I was aware of the predominantly Black areas of town—Walnut Hills, Over-the-Rhine, Avondale, and I was aware of other neighborhoods populated by poor and working class whites, many of whom had migrated to Ohio from Kentucky or West Virginia. And then, of course, the predominately white and affluent suburbs.

I knew that when I drove through Over-the-Rhine to get to various social service agencies downtown or to pick up a client, it was not uncommon to notice someone openly wielding a gun or to spot sex workers soliciting business in the broad daylight. I knew that it was an economically disadvantaged part of the city, with high rates of violent crime and drug sales, and I knew that it was best to stay in my car and keep moving.

What I did not know, for instance, was that fourteen African-Americans had died in confrontations with Cincinnati police between 1995 and March of 2001. I didn't know that early in 2001, the American Civil Liberties Union and local Black activists had filed a federal racial profiling suit against the Cincinnati Police Department, citing decades of discriminatory behavior. The Cincinnati City Council had subsequently adopted a law to address racial profiling, which required CPD officers to record the details of every traffic stop they made. Even when Timothy Thomas, an unarmed nineteen-year-old Black man, was killed by Officer Stephen Roach in downtown Cincy on the night of April 7, 2001, I still didn't understand the context of this horror. Not the way I do now—post-Trayvon Martin, post-Michael Brown, post-George Floyd, post-Brianna Taylor, post-Sandra Bland.

I was twenty-three years old, working my first full-time job, and I found myself living just north of where the so-called "race riots" broke out in downtown Cincinnati. My first apartment was a studio at Tudor Court Apartments, a single historic building with hardwood floors, crown molding, and ample character. I lived on Ludlow Avenue, a quaint street on the north side of the University of Cincinnati campus. The street was punctuated with old-fashioned black lamp-posts, a perfect spot for strolling the sidewalks, which were lined with eclectic shops and local businesses. There was Sitwell's—an early locus of coffee-shop culture, the independent bookstore where I first encountered the progressive Christian writings of John Shelby Spong, both Indian and Thai restaurants, a jewelry store with sterling silver items handmade by Indigenous artists, a Graeter's ice cream shop, and an IGA grocery store—all within walking distance. I could even go on foot to the local LGBTQ-affirming Methodist church just a few blocks away. Ludlow was a little bit of heaven for artists, intellectuals, and those with lifestyles alternative to the mainstream. I still have a book on relationships and astrology, called *Sex Signs*, gifted to me by a woman who lived in my building. She was the first openly transgender person I'd ever met, and we bonded over late-night conversation in the laundry room. I never saw her again.

When Timothy Thomas died that night by a single gunshot wound to the heart, in a dark alley off Vine Street, he was being chased by an off-duty officer who recognized him as a citizen with outstanding warrants. Fourteen outstanding warrants, to be exact, but all for misdemeanors and traffic offenses. He had no violent criminal history, and I repeat, no gun. By Monday April 9, protestors had gathered outside of City Hall and police headquarters, demanding answers. According to the *Cincinnati Enquirer*, by April 10 *"civil unrest turned more violent. Protesters overturned planters and hot dog stands, broke windows and pulled several white motorists from their cars and assaulted them. By day's end, police had arrested 66 people, including five juveniles, and the Cincinnati Fire Divi-*

sion made 53 runs. Eleven fires, most minor, were set in Over-the-Rhine."

The violence continued to escalate over the next two days as the uprising gained strength and protests spread into other predominantly Black areas of the city. The US Department of Justice sent in a team to consider a civil rights investigation against CPD. The mayor and governor strategized over what to do, and finally, on Thursday April 12, Mayor Charlie Luken declared a state of emergency and imposed a citywide curfew from 8 pm until 6 am. The curfew lasted four nights and finally brought a superficial rest to the city.

On the afternoon of April 12, I had an appointment with one of my youngest clients. He was 18 or 19, I can't recall, and still lived with his parents and younger siblings in a neighborhood on the edge of downtown. Kevin, a gentle soft-spoken young Black man, had a diagnosis of schizophrenia and was due for a checkup with his psychiatrist. I picked him up in my silver Toyota Camry, as usual, and accompanied him to see his doctor. But on the journey home, we took a detour. As we pulled onto a street still several blocks from his house, Kevin asked me to pull over.. "I don't think it's safe for you to go any further. It'll be better if you drop me off here and head away from downtown." I don't recall him adding the qualifier, "since you are a white woman driving into a predominantly Black neighborhood that is reeling from yet another homicide at the hands of a white police officer," but it was implied. I didn't argue, and I thanked him for looking out for me. Kevin was not an emotionally expressive or effusive person; his flat affect may have stemmed largely from his illness or perhaps the medication used to treat it. But that afternoon his kindness consumed the space between us. It seemed that he was truly concerned for my safety and not just my comfort. It also was clear that Kevin was much more attuned to the realities of race in our city than I was. As a young black man, he had to be attuned to survive.

The following day, I drove to the airport to pick up my college roommate Clare, who had come all the way from North Carolina for a weekend visit. It was our first reunion since graduation, but instead of venturing out across the city to show her the nightlife, we spent our evenings under curfew, hunkered down in my cozy Ludlow apartment, while neighbors downtown rallied and grieved and raged.

Sometime in May of 2001, I left my job at QCM and took a position at The Respite Center, a short term treatment facility for the same type of clients I had served as a case manager. On my last visit with another client named James, who was barely eighteen, he knowingly handed me a brand new copy of a book on the practice of self-care. Inside I found the inscription, "I hope this helps you learn how to take care of yourself as well as you take care of your clients."

More than once my clients knew what I needed better than I did.

Chapter 16

Alternative Medicines

James was right; I had a lot to learn about caring for myself. About the time that Cincinnati was coming apart at the seams, reopening an old wound that had been festering under the surface for decades—a very similar thing was happening to me. After I started taking Prozac my senior year of college and seeing a psychologist at the Wake Forest campus counseling center, my depression gradually lifted. I was learning to take walks and adjust my diet to support better moods. I was learning to live with this old diagnosis in new ways. And, as with so many of my clients at QCM, once I started feeling better, I stopped taking the medication. Less than a year later, I found myself back in that miry, sinking pit of despair.

Part of it was situational—managing the treatment plans of seventy or eighty adults with severe mental illness would be difficult for just about anyone. Turnover was high among case managers at QCM. We all coped in different ways—caffeine, cigarettes, sugar, dark humor. While many of my colleagues would step outside for smoke breaks, I regularly walked over to the 7-11 next door for Mountain Dew and powdered donuts. And that was just breakfast. While I was at QCM, one of my teammates died by suicide. She was so lovely—she had the most gorgeous black curly hair that gently draped her shoulders. She kept her short nails painted and accessorized with chunky silver and turquoise rings and necklaces that paired perfectly with her olive skin. She was kind and funny, in a Seinfeld sort of way, and she loved to show us pictures of her two young children. She was divorced and trying to date again. I had no idea how much she had been suffering.

I remember lying awake some nights, anxious because I hadn't been able to find housing for this client or that. I got increasingly behind on my paperwork. We were required to keep extensive documentation of all our work—daily case notes on every phone call, visit, or outreach made to or on behalf of a client, plus treatment plans updated at regular intervals. Failure to complete the required documentation could jeopardize funding for the agency; it was that serious.

Before I left QCM and took a job at The Respite Center, my supervisor had every-so-gently let me know that my late paperwork would eventually put me at risk of losing my job. He let me know this around the same time he also gently encouraged me to get help for my own depression.

After several more years of suffering with depression that was at times debilitating, and after several years of individual therapy, going on and off medications, I began attending group therapy sessions with a collection of people who were living with PTSD. Post-traumatic Stress Disorder is not just for soldiers who have survived the horrors of war; it can arise after any type of traumatic event---a rape, any kind of abuse, and in my case, emotional abuse and the sudden and unanticipated loss of home. It was the first time that I realized leaving Zambia at age six and never getting to say goodbye was not just sad or difficult, but traumatic. What I had internalized from the experience is that the things we love most in life–the places, the people, the dreams–will one day be suddenly taken from us, without much warning and not even the chance to say a proper farewell.

Throughout my twenties, I searched for healing wherever I could find it—therapy, antidepressants, spiritual direction, prayer, music, romantic love and marriage—and they all played their part. I met my first husband, Drew, in the fall of 2021, when we were both doing mental health work in Cincinnati. We married in 2003 and moved to his home state of Texas in 2004, Austin to be exact.

The excitement of moving to a new city, especially one as vibrant and eclectic as Austin, lifted my mood for a while. I was accepted, on a full merit scholarship, to Austin Presbyterian Theological Seminary, where I felt affirmed, seen, and challenged in ways that allowed me to flourish academically and to begin finding my way toward a life in ministry. And then the sinking feeling came back again.

My mother-in-law at the time was seeing an acupuncturist for back pain. One day at her apartment, I ran across a brochure that described acupuncture as an effective treatment for depression. Weary of the weary feeling and feeling that I had tried virtually everything else, I made an appointment.

In Chinese medicine, the pulse is one of the most important vital signs, just as it is in Western medicine. But in Chinese medicine, there are at least 29 different pulse types, described as floating, scattered, hollow, deep, thready, slippery, wiry, long/short, tight, or soggy—just to name a few. The quality of the pulse, among other things, dictates the nature of the treatments. Turns out you can tell a lot about a person by how the blood flows through their veins.

For months I saw my acupuncturist, Kristina, weekly for

needle treatments, and I took herbal supplements in between. By the end of every treatment, I could quite literally feel the energy (the chi, as it is known) flowing through my body, bringing my organs and systems back into balance. That's what Chinese medicine is about: Restoring balance, so that our inner ecosystems have the capacity to support health and ward off illness. It's about understanding that the bacteria in your gut affect the balance in your brain, for example.

This insight, that the environment, whether it be the one inside of you or the one outside of you, can be either conducive to health or susceptible to disease is not just a medical one. Its spiritual meaning is just as deep. And so it was that my depression did lift after months of weekly treatments and spiritual work on my insides; eighteen months later I had experienced a resurrection of sorts. And yet, while my inner peace soared, the ecosystem of my marriage was on the verge of collapse.

Chapter 17

White Weave

"Do the best you can until you know better. Then when you know better, do better."
~Maya Angelou

IN 2007 I MADE MY FIRST PILGRIMAGE BACK HOME TO Zambia since 1989, when I was 11 years old. I traveled with a group of fellow seminarians for an educational and cultural exchange with Zambian theology students at Justo Mwale University in Lusaka. On that same trip in 2007, I decided to get a hair weave. I feel like that sentence itself sounds absurd. White hair, or at least my fine, flat white hair, is not meant to be weaved. But you have probably seen photos of young white women returning from African vacations or short-term mission trips, with one or two beaded braids as a souvenir of their exotic adventures. Merchant hair stylists linger on the beaches of Mombasa, Kenya, for example, offering this 'authentic' African experience for a meager fee.

My 2007 trip back to Zambia was a fraught one. Delightful and fulfilling in many respects, it also heightened my awareness that the location of 'home' is elusive for me. Having not been in the country for eighteen years, I felt like a foreigner, unambiguously American. Yet the land itself was not completely foreign *to me*, and this familiarity set me apart from the American colleagues journeying with me. When we arrived in Lusaka and made our way from the airport through the city, certain districts and stretches of terrain were familiar.

It is difficult to describe what, precisely, I recognized; many of my Zambia memories are pre-verbal. Yet the tree-lined medians down major thoroughfares, the white-walled compounds marking off residential areas, and the unfinished dirt roads in other parts emerged like snapshots from my psyche. I also noticed what had not been there two decades before---billboards bearing the images of American preachers, like T.D. Jakes and various purveyors of the prosperity Gospel. Chinese business development. Cell phones everywhere.

I decided to get the full hair weave because I felt that one or two braids was appropriate for a tourist or a visitor, and I was not a tourist. I may not be Indigenous, but I also would not be merely a tourist.

This is the predicament of all kinds of third culture kids: We are not one thing or the other. We exist somewhere in the middle. In my case, I live in the center of the Venn diagram where Zambia and the US overlap. It is a narrow space, not well-defined, and frequently I topple over into one side or the other.

In order to achieve a full set of braids, I sat with a Zambian woman for four or five hours, while her nimble fingers compelled my natural hair to conform to the strands of synthetic hair I had purchased at the open air market, deep in the heart of a nearby village. My colleague Ruth, who happened to be a hair stylist back in Texas, took me on the excursion into the village and helped me find hair that matched my shade of reddish brown. That shopping trip itself was immersive.

To get to the village, we left the seminary compound at Justo Mwale and started down the wide dirt road that ran parallel. I recall taking a left turn down another more narrow dirt road that moved along the edge of the village. Homes began to dot the roadside to our right. Simple homes. Perhaps of cinder block or wood. Thatched or tin roofs. Toddlers and school-age children emerged from the doorways. Some yelled, "Mzungu!" (white person!) as we passed. They laughed; I think from both joy and amusement. We smiled and waved, keeping our forward momentum. I don't recall seeing a single other white person in the village or the market. Ruth, being African-American, was not so obtrusive as me, but I must have been a sight.

Finally a right turn into the village center. The market itself was makeshift. Small stalls delineated by walls of wooden poles tied together. Cloth or weather-proof tarps for roofing. And each unit devoted to a different ware---produce, clothing, hygiene, electronics, freshly slaughtered chickens, and beauty. We weaved ourselves between stalls and fellow shoppers until we found a nook devoted to hair.

I relished this departure from the itinerary that had been set for us. I even skipped out on a planned event, to the slight annoyance of my professor, to have my hair done.

The young Zambian woman who agreed to braid my hair was the wife of a student at the seminary, so she came to the seminary guest rooms, where my colleagues from the US and I were staying. While the other Americans were away, I sat cross-legged on the floor against the edge of a bed. She sat behind me.

I asked questions about her life:

How often do you do hair?

Tell me about your children.
Do you like living here at the seminary?
How does your husband enjoy his classes?

She asked me questions about my life in the US. I don't remember what they were. To my embarrassment, I cannot even remember her name. We had only this one afternoon together. Most of the time we were not even face-to-face.

What I have not forgotten is how painful the experience was. That memory is visceral. She tugged and twisted; my tender scalp smarted and squirmed. For days I was adjusting to the tension in my forehead. On occasion it itched:

Does it always hurt this badly?
Is it because my scalp is virginal in this regard? Or because my hair is so slippery and fine?
How do Black women in the US endure this torture so regularly?
Only to be told when they get to the office that their hair is too "ethnic" to be professional?

I was determined, though, not to complain. Because what was painful to my body was healing to my soul. I felt so thoroughly grateful to sit in such intimate proximity to a Zambian woman. To sit in both silence and conversation, alternately. To invite her hands on my head to restore something to my heart, a thing that had been lost decades earlier when my family returned to the US prematurely. Until the age of 6, most of my best friends were Black Zambians. And then suddenly, at age 6, they were white Americans. The sense of grief I felt and still feel is not only that I lost best friends, but that I also lost my welcome in a Zambian community. I have always understood that I am not Black, but there was a time when I felt Zambian.

For four or five hours in that dorm room salon, I felt Zambian again.

I made sure that I compensated her fairly. On the one hand, this was primarily an economic exchange. But for me it was a therapy, a blessing, a homecoming. Indeed, in Zambian culture, braiding hair is one of the primary ways that women and girls take care of each other. It is what they do together between performing the many domestic chores that consume most of their time. It is a ritual of love, belonging, and feminine worth.

Looking back I am most struck by how full of grace and generosity the whole encounter was. I am not sure what Ruth, or Kim (the other African-American woman on our trip), or my Zambian stylist actually thought about this white woman in a full set of braids. But Ruth was the one who offered to help me buy the hair at the market, and once it was done, she taught me how to wash my new hair; she showed me how to tie back the braids, and eventually I purchased two scarves for that purpose---one a pale blue and the other white with Black leopard print. I remember Ruth saying it was a strong, sexy look for me, that my husband back home would be thrilled.

At the time no one made me feel absurd for trying to coax my white hair into a Black mode. It seemed they were gentle with my longing for a physical connection to my Zambian home. The way Ruth, in particular, responded is remarkable to me now because of my growing awareness of the history of appropriation, specifically that of white women appropriating the styles of African and African-American women, with little to no appreciation for the roots, pun intended, of these styles. Think Bo Derrick in *Ten*. And more recently Rachel Dolezal, who not only wears the braids but claims the African heritage as her own. Correction: Not just the heritage, also the skin color; Rachel Dolezal says she is Black.

For all I know, Ruth thought I was making an insensitive, even racist, choice when you consider the ways Black women in the US have been persecuted and policed because of their hair. My sense, in retrospect, is that her pride in both her cultural heritage and her profession drove Ruth to take the position that if I was going to do this thing with my hair, she would make sure I did it right. Whatever her private opinion, the result was that she helped me preserve the integrity of the braids for as long as possible.

Still. The truth is that whenever a white woman wears an African look, no matter how well-intentioned, it can never be "just a hairstyle." The impact of her choice will inevitably show up multi-layered. At the time I wore my weave, I initially did not feel conspicuous, though surely I was…until we left Zambia and arrived in Cape Town.

~

I could feel the stares as soon as we got off the plane.

Imagine Cape Town at night. A dimly-lit restaurant in a wooded spot. White tablecloths, extensive wine list, and springbok on the menu. Mostly white dinner companions, too, save Ruth, Kim, a Black gentleman, and our student guide who was mixed race, or "coloured," as he was called growing up in apartheid South Africa.

This is one side of Cape Town, inhabited by white Afrikaners, many of them wealthy, at least by comparison to the Black South Africans who live in nearby shanty towns. In these townships, homes constructed of colorful red, blue, and silver tin are crowded onto the hillsides. Squat structures in lengthy rows. Some are lucky enough to have functioning electricity, but indoor plumbing is a rarity. In some cases, a shanty town settlement can be found just across the street from neighborhoods exclusive to the rich---towering stone mansion monstrosities defiantly oblivious to the people who dwell in their shadow.

Consider that for decades it was illegal for white and Black South Africans to intermarry. Their "coloured" children were evidence of a crime, as Trevor Noah describes in his own memoir. In some respects, mixed race South Africans were treated better than Black South Africans, but they still received far less resources, education, and status than whites.

Now imagine a white woman in full African braids blurring the color lines in this context:

On which side of the street should she reside?

How much privilege does a white woman need to wear Black hair without fear of reprisal, in this country where the mixing of races has been both personally and politically dangerous?

How tone deaf does she need to be not to perceive how freely she moves, in a country where Black and mixed race people still, even in the post-apartheid years, yearn for freedom in its fullness?

During our stay in South Africa, we spent a great deal of time with our student guide. I found him polite and professional always, but I also found him cautious and perhaps even suspicious with me, in a way that I did not observe in his interactions with others. He never commented on my hair, so what I am about to say may be purely projection. (I am an intuitive person, but that does not make me a mind-reader, I know.) In the decade since that trip, I have come to wonder whether my white weave was an affront to his lifetime of navigating the precarious space between races, without ever having a choice. Surely one of the key features of freedom is the privilege to choose---something I have in spades.

Days later, I recall gliding down the escalator in the airport in Austin, Texas, spotting the man who is now my ex-husband standing expectantly at the bottom. The backdrop to all of this was a strained marriage that would ultimately collapse in about eight months time. I smiled. He stared, noticeably perplexed by my hair. We went directly to lunch from the airport. I was hungry and exhausted from the transatlantic journey home. Then we drove back to our seminary apartment on 30th street. We had sex before he left for his evening shift at the cigar shop. Maybe Ruth was right about the hair? Strong and sexy. But in the days that followed, whenever we went out in public together, what I intuited from him was discomfort. One of the city's mottos is "Keep Austin Weird;" surely I was doing my part. But he needed me to be weird in a whiter way, more south Austin hippie/hipster, less ethnic, less African, less in-between.

When it comes to drawing a line between cultural appreciation and cultural appropriation, not everyone agrees on where the demarcation should be. But there seems to be consensus that appropriation happens when white people adopt the expressions of an oppressed culture (hairstyles, foods, fashions, musical genres, language, religious traditions, etc.) without awareness of the cultural significance of these forms and without concern for the dignity of the people who have gifted the world with the very things we covet.

To the extent that 2007 me was still ignorant about the ways hair carries both meaning and a history of discrimination in African, and especially African-American culture, I believe my white weave was a form of appropriation. My intentions were pure, but intent is only part of the equation. Impact matters more. And this can be a hard lesson for people with privilege, but we *can* learn.

Chapter 18

What Makes You a Whore

[Flashback] The Lake House, 1996

I can still see my father leaning against the pale blue kitchen counter at our home on Graham St. in Greenville, North Carolina. Senior prom is around the corner, and it's a really big deal. I almost feel popular this year. Phil finally asked me to be his date. I've found a sequined dress, with multi-colored pieces put together like a jigsaw puzzle. It's edgy and sparkly and one-of-a-kind. My hair finally is long enough for a French braid. AND we've been invited to Alison's house for a fancy meal with a big group of friends. It's tradition for these friends to head out of town after prom and spend the night at Chris' lake house. Yes, there will be underage drinking. Yes, these are a bunch of privileged upper middle class white kids. And, yes, just this once I want to do what the popular kids do.

Please, Mom. Please, Dad.

"If you go to that after party, people will think you're a whore," my father snarled.

"Ellis!" my Mom barked back.

The conversation pretty much ended there, but several days later, presumably after behind-the-scenes negotiations between my parents, I was allowed to go to the after prom party at the lake house.

Turns out the party was a little overrated. Phil ended up getting really drunk off the "purple Jesus" punch, and my best friend Leslie and I bore witness while he puked, then got him safely to a bed to sleep it off. Leslie and I stayed sober for the full duration of the night, keeping tabs on the others, and staying high off the sheer adventure of being allowed this night away from home.

Turns out everybody knew I wasn't a whore.

[Flashback] Riverside Drive, 2008

I had found them outside the cigar shop, thinking I would catch him alone, shutting down for the night after his shift. They were seated next to the sidewalk—my first husband Drew and his coworker Erica, focused intently on one another, their faces just inches apart.

I approached and spoke directly, "Would someone like to tell me what's going on here?"

"Nothing," she shrugged.

I knew in my bones that this was a lie. I had known it for months. I had suspected something awry at Christmastime, and on New Year's Eve when I returned from sweat lodge to find the two of them in a similar fashion, faces and bodies just inches apart, standing at the back of the walk-in humidor.

I had felt it in my bones on the day in February when he announced that he was leaving, when he sat beside me on the bed we shared in our apartment, revealing the awful truth of his infidelity—that he had cheated on me in the very first year of our marriage, and approximately once every year after, for the five years we had been married. I had specifically asked if something was going on with *her*, with Erica and he had said no. But even then, I knew in my bones that it was a lie.

I now know the term "gaslighting," but at the time, I felt crazy. All of the evidence before my eyes and the intuitions of my heart told one truth, while my husband told a singular lie---that there was nothing going on.

"I know that's not true." Back outside the cigar shop I spoke up, rage and insistence rising to the surface, what I knew in my bones erupting to the level of skin.

She walked toward me, "You're fucking crazy!" she retorted.

I raised my fist and reared back, meeting resistance only when my husband raised his hand to grab my arm and block the blow. It was one of the last times he touched me. And it was a singular moment in time. When you have been living a lie for years and your body finally knows the truth in its bones, your own viscera will do whatever they can to protect your wisdom. I had almost punched her in the face, and it was a sign of healing.

∽

That night I went back to my friend Ann's house, where I had been staying for several weeks after moving out of the apartment I had shared with my husband. At the time, he and I had agreed to an intentional separation, during which time he would consider whether he wanted to continue being married and ultimately work to reconcile. The big caveat was that, during this mere month of separation, if he cheated on me again, I would immediately move toward divorce. His continued infidelity would be his clearest answer to the question.

A few days before, I had returned to my old apartment to retrieve a few more of my belongings. There I had discovered my husband's checkbook lying open on the dining room table, exposing a new address in an apartment complex off Riverside Drive. I had a very strong suspicion that he had moved in with her.

The morning after the confrontation at the cigar shop, I awoke before dawn, having been plagued by restlessness in the night. It must have been around 6am. Foregoing a shower, I threw on clothes, brushed my teeth, and headed toward downtown Austin as the sun peeked over the horizon. I drove south on I-35 with a determination I have felt only a few times in my life, compelled by what I only know to describe as the Spirit of God. Let me tell you what I mean by that. I am not talking about some kind of "manifest destiny" propelling me westward to conquer "new" land and ancient peoples. I did not hear an audible voice dictating instructions! I'm talking about that thing, that inner voice, that energy inside us all that resists colonization by whatever or whoever is trying to suck the life out of us, be it by brute force or cowardly lies.

As I said, I drove south, trying to salvage my dignity and recover my lifeforce. At Riverside Drive I exited, following my phone's mapping app to the address listed in that checkbook. As I approached the apartment complex, I noticed the locked entry gate and felt momentarily deflated, but I steeled my resolve and fumbled in my mind for a backup plan. By a stroke of either luck or grace, a car inside the complex came from behind the back building and approached the gate to exit, so I pulled in quickly after him and casually parked in an inconspicuous spot near the entrance.

This is where the real sleuthing began. The address in the checkbook had left off the specific apartment number. I had no idea how I would find her, now *their*, actual apartment. Part

The Water and the Blood, the Blood and the Water

scorned woman and part PI, I stepped out of my car and approached a large courtyard, with four sides around a central swimming pool. Several floors of individual living units on every side of the pool, each marked by red door after red door. Where would I even begin?

I texted Drew to let him know I was on the property. No response.

It was just past 7am now, and I wasn't certain how many renters would even be awake, but shortly, I caught a glimpse of an older woman through her first floor window. I cleared my throat and knocked gently. She opened the door momentarily, offering a bright smile and wondering how she could help.

I explained that I was looking for my friend Erica's apartment. I had visited her before and could not, for the life of me, remember the apartment number, and I had been texting her but no answer. Some of that was true. A little bit.

Perhaps this is the right moment to mention that the ethics of this whole endeavor were muddled, to say the least. What I knew in that moment was that I had to know the truth and that my husband could not be trusted to tell it to me. I would need to see it with my own eyes if I was ever going to feel sane and free.

So I persisted. That lovely neighbor thought for a moment. She could not tell me the exact apartment, but she thought there was an Erica who lived in the section of apartments on "this" side of the pool, gesturing to the side on my right. I thanked her kindly and followed the sidewalk in the direction she had pointed.

Only a few red doors down, something miraculous happened. There was my dog, Niko, the one I shared with my husband at the time, barking and bouncing and practically smiling in recognition of my presence. I saw Niko's face through the first-floor window, but no human came in response to his barking. The thing I did next I did without much thinking at all. I opened the door. I opened the door to someone else's apartment to get to my dog. I'm not sure if the miracle is that the door was unlocked, or if the miracle is that I so nonchalantly waltzed right in. That last part was probably more criminal than miracle, but it is a thing I, in fact, did. And the truth is, the Spirit within that seeks Life is not always deterred by constructs like legality, civility, and obedience.

As I stepped into the bottom floor of what I now realized was a two-story townhome, two more dogs bounded down the stairway toward Niko and myself, and I looked up to find Drew standing there, completely nude, at the top of the stairs.

I think both of us were in shock. He was in shock to see me standing there, and I was in shock that my plan had worked. He was terrified, and I was, for the first time in years, finally relieved.

"What are you doing here?" he asked nervously.

"What are YOU doing here?" I retorted. "Put some clothes on, Erica. I'm coming up!" I warned as I marched defiantly up the stairs. I felt like the grown up in the situation, confronting two children found in the act of some forbidden activity.

"How do you even know we live here?" she asked incredulously.

At the top of the stairs now, standing in a triangle with Erica and my ex, I reported that I had found the address in a checkbook that her "boyfriend" had left on the dining room table in the apartment he still technically shared with me.

As Drew searched frantically for his underwear, I went on, "Erica, you of all people should know better than to sleep with another woman's husband! After what your mother did to your father!"

When I am angry, I am quick-witted, and my words can be biting. It is a quality of which I am not particularly proud, but in that moment, after years of second-guessing my sanity, I had found my voice and was not backing down. Because I knew Erica, I knew that her mother had left her father for another man years before, leaving him to care for her and her brother as a single dad. Less than three months before this confrontation, I had invited Erica and her father into our home for Christmas dinner. I had unwittingly served a fucking pot roast to my husband's mistress, and I was not backing down.

"You of all people should know better!" I accused her.

Half-dressed, she put her hands to her hips, cocked her head to one side, and said casually, "I don't care."

"And that's what makes you a whore," I said calmly in return.

"That's what makes you a whore." Not your sensuality or your sexuality. Not going to prom after-parties or wearing provocative clothing, or even making your living in the sex industry. What makes you, what makes anyone, a whore is not caring about the people you hurt along the way to gratifying your own desires.

Erica now quickly demanded that I leave the premises, threatening to call the police if I did not oblige. I had invaded her space and was eager to escape that ugly scene, so I hurried to leave, but not before I instructed Drew to get dressed. "You're coming with me," I explained.

We had things to sort out and sort through, divorce proceedings to initiate, and a few final lies to expose. Lest anyone think that I primarily blamed Erica for my husband's infidelity, be assured that I knew him to be the biggest whore of all. He had lied to me for years and manipulated me into thinking that I was insecure and paranoid every time I became suspicious that he was being unfaithful.

He made it out of the house dressed but shoeless, emblematic of his humiliation. I was so used to feeling humiliated and powerless in our marriage that I felt a sense of justice and vindication in that moment. But far more than taking joy in anyone else's suffering, I mostly felt utterly relieved. For the first time in years, I knew I wasn't fucking crazy. I had the evidence, the proof.

CHAPTER 19

THE PULSE

IT IS EVER-TEMPTING TO MAKE OURSELVES THE heroes of our own stories. I could easily be the hero of my divorce. A woman scorned. The victim of infidelity. It is true that I did not deserve so much of the way I was treated in my first marriage, especially in the end. I say this plainly because for so long I believed it was my fault

In reality almost all marriages fail because of a combination of factors that cannot be located solely within one person. For most of the early years of my first marriage, I was clinically depressed and finding my way out of it. Later Drew would encounter his own depression and despair. We each held layers of unresolved trauma, and we both were engaged in the complex process of deconstructing the religious upbringings of our childhoods.

We both came up in conservative Christian traditions that gave us very few tools for grappling with sexuality. We essentially were taught to repress desire until marriage and then given very little guidance about how to unleash that power after we had made our vows. I have seen over and over again, in my personal life and in my pastoral work, how repression breeds shame, secrecy, and distortion and puts up roadblocks to intimacy. You even see this in the broader American society, with its pendulum swinging between purity culture and the porn industry.

Depression, religious deconstruction, desire---these were the kindling for a passion that burned hot and then burned out of control. We could not sustain that kind of intensity. We loved each other the best we could with the tools we had at the time, and although the divorce was excruciatingly painful, the marriage also became an incubator for the better people we could become. In the end it broke, and it broke us open and set us on a broader path toward wholeness.

In the aftermath of it all, I've pretty much given up on the notion of either heroes or whores. If what makes you a whore is not caring about the people you hurt along the way to gratifying your own desires, and what makes you a hero is living your life in sacrificial service to others, most of us are neither one or the other. We are a little bit of both.

What I can tell you is that about a year after I found Drew & Erica in that townhouse with the red door, I finally got my pulse back...

Chapter 20

Tangled Roots

[Flashback] It is April 4, 2018, 50 years to the day that the Rev. Dr. Martin Luther King, Jr. was assassinated in Memphis. I am standing in line at the Museum of African-American History and Culture, just adjacent to the Washington Monument along the National Mall in DC. It is a free day at the museum, and families, many of them African-American, are flooding the plaza to make their way into the exhibits.

You begin in the dark underbelly of a slave ship and voyage gradually into the light of day as you ascend to each higher level of the museum. The journey from darkness to light mimics the historic journey from slavery toward freedom.

I am lucky that my group doesn't have to wait long. After a brief orientation, we descend into the lower level of the museum and begin to journey from the earliest days of the transAtlantic slave trade, through the Civil War, Jim Crow South, Civil Rights Era, and finally into the 21st century and a celebration of Black culture---music, athletics, theatre.

On the lower level, it is noticeably dark. The spaces are cramped, and only the photos and texts of the exhibits are well-illuminated. It is a free day, and it is crowded, bodies packing in tightly, inching forward slowly. In the display cases, history unfolds---details about the African countries where slaves were gathered, details about the dangerous conditions aboard the 'cargo' ships that carried them.

I overhear a conversation between a mother and her elementary age daughter:

"Mommy, were they trying to kill these people on the boats?"

"No, baby, they needed them to get here alive so they could work."

No, they needed them to get here alive so they could work.

I try to keep moving forward, taking in as much information as I can, but realize my progress is painfully slow. There are so many people in the space that the air seems thin, and I feel claustrophobic. I want to get to higher ground. And then I remember that the architecture is designed to evoke precisely this kind of experience.

I expected to be challenged and inspired by this symbolic journey; I am caught off guard by how much I feel it in my body. The images of Africa don't feel like distant historical artifacts to me; they're like reminders of home. They conjure up memories and images of my own. I can hear the guttural, rhythmic sounds of Zambian church choirs singing and dancing; it is like no other sound on Earth. I hear the roar of Victoria Falls and taste sweet mango on my tongue.

But I am not Black. I am not the descendant of slaves. I scan the crowd at the museum, wondering if the hundreds of African-American patrons feel this sense of connection to the motherland, or if they only feel the loss of home and alienation from their origins. I feel conspicuous---why should this white woman have an intimate sense of Africa, when so many Black Americans have never stepped foot on African soil?

But I do know Africa in my body. The reason I do is because I was born there to missionary parents. Because even though Zambia had gained political independence by the time my parents arrived there, my parents still were carrying on the legacy of colonialist missionary work focused on converting Indigenous people to Christianity. No doubt my parents' approach was more compassionate and culturally-sensitive than many historical approaches to this conversion project, but it is all part of one long trajectory. I carry that colonialist past in my body, too.

In my body, Africa feels like unspoiled freedom. Also in my flesh is the knowledge that I was lucky enough to taste this freedom in childhood because white people went before me and took control over bodies and lands that did not belong to them. Many people lost freedom so that I could have more.

"Tangled Roots." That's what our Springtime trip to DC and the MAAHC was called---a pilgrimage of tangled roots. The title points to the complex of racism, theology, and politics that has been convoluting the American freedom dream since our earliest days as a collection of colonies. How can we ever heal as a country from the original sin of chattel slavery without somehow untangling these root systems?

But the tangled roots are not just out there in our social, political, and ecclesiastical institutions, the complexity and confusion is planted firmly within our individual psyches. Or at least this is true of me. My mother has long referred to me as her "African baby." And I am. I claim this and love this about who I am. I also am the child of Whiteness, conversion, saviors, and subtle, benevolent racism. This I do not love.

Chapter 21

Born For Free

My mother recalls that I was the only white baby in the nursery the night I was born. She wasn't really even supposed to be using that hospital. Officially, it was a facility devoted solely to copper miners and their families. But my mother had come under the care of a British physician affiliated with the hospital, and when it was time for her to deliver, the mining hospital was, essentially, the only option in the rural part of Zambia where we lived. Because my father was not a miner, and we were not actually supposed to be there, no bill was issued. And the doctor did not charge her, so my mother loves to say that I was born for free.

It *is* remarkable when you consider the cost of giving birth in most American hospitals. Often I have pondered what it might mean to be born 'for free,' whether there is some kind of spiritual value to starting life without your existence immediately being monetized and commodified. Surely the answer is yes.

In retrospect, I wonder to what extent it was my mother's social location---her whiteness, her status as an American---that gained her access into the mining hospital, more so than any one doctor's generosity. I trust that he was generous; it's just that two things can be true at the same time. People can be kind and generous and still be operating with personal prejudice and within biased systems that cater to some people over others. It happens all the time. I wonder if the tables were turned, for example, and a Black Zambian miner and his wife had sought care from a physician that generally treated foreign diplomats, wealthy government officials, or American ex-patriots, I wonder if the healthcare hospitality extended would have been the same. Could their poorer Black child have been born 'for free'?

Perhaps a better question is what does it cost to live 'for free'? In America some patriots are fond of saying that "freedom isn't free." Of course what they don't tell you is that often those who pay the most get the least amount of freedom in return. Like the Black soldiers who fought in WWII, only to face Jim Crow laws in the South and redlining in the North, when they came home to the "land of the free." Or like contemporary veterans of the US military who are also immigrants and have faced deportation under the current administration's obsession with "making America great (i.e. white) again."

For me the real gift of being born in Zambia is not so much being born for free, but rather being born into a pre-American kind of freedom. I recall Zambia as an Eden; Africa is, after all, the cradle of humanity. In my psyche, Zambia represents that unspoiled archetypal freedom experienced by Adam and Eve, our mythical father and mother---the kind of freedom that exists prior to all the evils and the -isms, which come along with having too much knowledge and too little wisdom to wield it well.

The Water and the Blood, the Blood and the Water

When I think of freedom, categories begin to cluster for me, and I wonder: What *does* it cost to be free?

These are what I think of as the fundamental freedoms, the bare minimum of liberty that one might expect to enjoy in a representative democracy. Assuming, of course, that you are not a slave (or perhaps a woman, or transgender, if we are talking about the USA in 2024):

Bodily freedom
Emotional freedom
Intellectual freedom
Political freedom
Spiritual freedom

Then there are what I am calling the "freedoms of privilege," the extras that seem to accumulate relative to one's level of wealth and power in a society. Most of these are a function of some degree of economic security:

The freedom to make choices
The freedom to fail and recover
The freedom to rest and try again

And then there are the freedoms even privilege cannot buy:

Freedom from oppression by one's own religious group
Freedom from systemic racism
Freedom from materialism

My family returned to the US in 1984, with the plan of taking a year-long furlough to help settle my older sister in her first year of college. Ultimately my parents decided not to go back to the mission field. Three of my grandparents were terminally ill, and there were other factors that evaded my awareness as a six-year-old. What I knew is that we weren't going back home, and I never got to say a proper goodbye.

A little bit of my liberty died that year. It was as if I had been banished from the Garden, except I had never tasted the forbidden fruit. What I noticed was the gradual loss of freedom---freedom of movement, freedom of expression, the freedom of not knowing what I didn't know.

There was no more dancing in church, as there had been every Sunday morning in the village church on Kalwa Farm. There was only dancing when my Mom and I gave our missionary presentation on Zambia to various congregations, and we danced up the aisles of sanctuaries around North Carolina, like live curios. How sad for them that the dance was a special performance and not a regular part of their ritual of worship.

There were no more Black best friends, except for a couple of years when we first moved to Taylorsville. But even then Toshia and I were an odd couple, and we learned to segregate soon enough.

There was no more ignorance about "stuff", meaning the material objects that take up so much space in the American psyche.

I have a foggy memory of walking into a shopping mall for the first time, oblivious to the fact that the goods enshrined there could be purchased and taken home. I was overwhelmed by it all and unaware that I needed anything, except to go home and be free again. Home to the place where chewing gum was so hard to come by that one year for Christmas, the most extravagant thing I could think to ask for was two packs of gum. Two packs, not one. And when I received this gift, I savored it for the year to come.

I remember taking a journey inward, to where I thought I could be safer and more protected from the grief of losing home. And in the process, I locked up anger and sadness and with them an exuberance that defined my early years in Zambia. I spoke my mind less, I tried to contain my body more. To be quiet and still, as I thought children in America were expected to be.

For me, America is not the land of the free. It is a land where being white and Christian and upper middle class can buy you a lot of things your soul doesn't need. It is a land for the "yearning to breathe free," a land freer than many, but also a land in bondage to the many -isms.

It is a land haunted by the *memory* of freedom as much as the practice. A memory that lives in the soil, recalling a time when First Nations cultivated and cared for the land. A precolonial memory, for sure. And perhaps even a pre-verbal one. A memory that lives in the collective unconscious, recalling Eden---the Garden from whence our restless souls came and long to go home again.

Chapter 22

The World House

(missionary work and the white savior complex)

"He had a wellspring of kindness in him, but also an incredible arrogance."
~ Petina Gappah, Zimbabwean author, speaking on the legacy of David Livingstone

When I was born, my family lived in the small city of Kitwe, but shortly after, we moved to a rural area near the town of Serenje, to Kalwa Farm. Kalwa Farm was donated to the Zambian Baptist Mission in 1971 by relatives of the 19th century British explorer and missionary David Livingstone. My family moved to the farm to join another missionary family, The Waddills, who lived in the old brick farmhouse where the Moffats, descendants of Livingstone's wife Mary, had originally made their home.

Kalwa was a working farm, managed by the Waddills---Uncle Tom and Aunt Lucille---from that old house. Tom and Lucille were not my blood relatives but functioned as family and, besides my own parents and siblings, were (along with their children) the only other non-Zambians residing on the property.

The house, completed in 1939, is a large brick home in a classic colonial style, although not nearly as big as I remember it in my childhood mind's eye. I do remember that it was the center of life on the farm, and so many of my earliest memories coalesce in scenes both outside and inside that structure.

[Snapshot] My gorgeous mother is posed on the front steps of the farmhouse, dressed in a lavender sari gifted to her by Indian friends, for what occasion I'm not sure. She is standing there before a long covered porch with her salt-n-pepper hair and inviting smile. The image conjures up the smell of hot samosas wrapped in a greasy brown paper sack and filled with spicy lamb, also a gift from our Indian friends.

[Snapshot] My best friend Ruth, with skin like velvet midnight and close-cropped hair, wears a bright yellow dress the color of crayon suns. She twirls about in the front yard, with the farmhouse as her backdrop. Then the scene shifts, and we sit together in the dirt playing jacks and other games whose rules I don't remember.

[Snapshot] Angela, Sheila, and I are crouched over a small tin can to one side of the home's interior courtyard, where we have tried to trap a small serpent so that later one of the Zambian men can come and relocate it to a more remote region of the farm. Everything is painted white, like a fresh canvas waiting for danger.

[Snapshot] Zambians are lined up in the outer courtyard, along the low red brick retaining wall, waiting for medical checks with Aunt Lucille. She scurries about, wide hips and white apron, equal parts authoritarian and saint. There are workers from the farm, older children, as well as nursing mothers whose infants are tied to them with chitengi cloth.

[Snapshot] In the main dining room, meat grinders are

mounted at intervals around a large wooden table. The adults will spend the day processing various cuts of meat from a freshly slaughtered cow.

[Snapshot] In that same dining room, we are gathered 'round for afternoon tea time—a colonial ritual, no doubt. Only there is no tea. We feast on dark chocolate and coconut Mounds(™) bars, washing it all down with bottled Coca-Cola. Tastes of America.

[Snapshot] Not far from the dining room, the Waddills and my family have gathered in the main living room. It is Christmastime, and the children have staged a scene in front of the large fireplace. I am approximately two years old, and I play Mary, perched on the back of my donkey, Howard, who is much older, probably in college at this point. I have only one line to deliver: "How can this be? For I am a virgin!" in response to the angel of God's pronouncement that I will give birth to the Messiah. But at showtime, I can't quite deliver. I am only two, after all. The angel speaks her good news again, and after a pregnant pause, I respond with confidence, "How can this be? For I am NOT a virgin!"

I loved that old house. Truth be told, I loved it more than my family's home. The walls seemed laden with memory and shimmering with wise ghosts. As a child, I thought I could get lost there, it felt so vast. Back staircases and hidden corridors, like secret passageways to the past. My own home was a newer, simpler construction. It was much more straightforward than the farmhouse, which has become for me an even greater paradox as I age.

I loved the farmhouse, in part, *because* it was old and because it was complicated. It had a history, beautiful and sordid. I also loved it because it was, aside from the simple village church, a gathering place upon which cultures and communities converged---to eat and laugh and pray and be healed. In retrospect, my mind and heart imagine it as an incarnation of The Rev. Dr. Martin Luther King, Jr.'s "World House," which King described in the following terms:

"Some years ago a famous novelist died. Among his papers was found a list of suggested plots for future stories, the most prominently underscored being this one: 'A widely separated family inherits a house in which they have to live together.' This is the great new problem of mankind. We have inherited a large house, a great "world house" in which we have to live together—black and white, Easterner and Westerner, Gentile and Jew, Catholic and Protestant, Moslem and Hindu—a family unduly separated in ideas, culture and interest, who, because we can never again live apart, must learn somehow to live with each other in peace."[1]

But the farmhouse is also an edifice built by colonialism. It is a representation of the white European's delusion that the world belongs, not to God, but to the white man, to conquer and to divide and possess and alter however he might see fit.

I've read that the Bemba tribe, the tribe with whom my father worked most closely in his missionary efforts, was matrilineal and matriarchal prior to the colonial period. The two factors that impinged upon this natural order of things were, firstly, the emergence of the British copper mining industry, which began to employ men in large numbers, drawing them away from domestic life and confining their wives to that sphere. And the second factor ---the patriarchal theology of western missionaries.

I had never heard this history of the Bemba people until a Google search (while writing this book) led me to anthropological sources on the internet, but it is not surprising that the

---

1. Martin Luther King, Jr,. from the chapter "The World House" in *Where Do We Go From Here: Chaos or Community*, 1967.

Christianity brought to Africa by western missionaries was indeed patriarchal and imperialistic, because it was those things back in the West from whence it came.

Christians often talk about the dangers of creating God in our own image, but of course this is so often precisely what we do. The particular danger of the Evangelical vision is not only to create God in our own image, but also to re-create the world in our image, too. The temptation is to think that we must make others resemble ourselves, in belief and practice, in order to find the divine image within them. When we give in to this temptation, we are likely to obscure the very aspects of the Other that have the most to teach us about God. Missionaries do this to varying degrees, on a spectrum from benevolent racism and Christocentrism to overt destruction and denigration of cultures.

There is no doubt in my mind that my father, and my mother with him, went to Zambia with some form of white savior complex, with the idea that their religion was superior to the animism and pantheism of traditional African religions. With the idea that their civilization was superior and their culture more advanced in the ways that really matter. David Livingstone, whose heart is quite literally buried in Zambia, thought he could end the slave trade by converting Africans to Christianity, thereby granting them greater human worth and dignity in the eyes of his British counterparts. Like Livingstone, my missionary parents believed that their work of converting the Zambian people to Christian faith would make the Zambians more acceptable in the sight of God and the West, that indeed it would save them.

Paired with this supremacy thinking, though, was something more humble---the idea that God had called them to sacrifice much of their own security and comfort to go into a part of the world that was indeed foreign to them and to bring with them into that unknown place the best of their resources, material and spiritual, to share. This posture of humility and vulnerability can, at its best, become the crucible for genuine relationships, collaboration, and cross-cultural learning. The best missionaries, in my opinion, end up finding themselves converted to something, too.

One of my favorite seminary professors, the one who had organized the trip to Zambia in 2007, wisely taught us that our Zambian hosts were savvy about finding a balance between graciously accepting the gifts and influences of Western Christians while also protecting their own self-determination. This insight exposes, I think, the supremacist thinking that both staunch defenders and unbending critics of missionary work tend to fall into. On the one hand, the apologists for Christian missionary work often assume that their African converts have accepted the Christian theologies of the West whole-cloth, that they have let go of all syncretistic ideas about God and all of their pantheist sensibilities, when in actuality most global Christians do a brilliant job of synthesizing Christian teachings with their own Indigenous beliefs and practices.

On the other hand, those who criticize all forms of missionary work, can also fall into the fallacy of thinking that global converts to Christianity are/were incapable of consciously choosing or refusing to adopt the new faith presented to them---that ALL conversions must have been forced. The assumptions on either side of this coin rob Indigenous people, in this case Zambians, of their agency. On both sides, it's West knows best, instead of the real life, complex, and nuanced experiences of actual Zambian people. In some contexts it is the traditional religions that have become oppressive, and Christianity is a freedom movement. In this way, there is no single thing that can truly be called Christianity. Expressions of Christian faith are ever and always contextual.

When it comes to the legacy of my own parents, my own family, well, it's complicated. I would do some, maybe many things, differently than my parents. I would not teach a theology that says believing in Jesus as Messiah is the only path to a literal heaven. I would not teach that homosexuality is sin. I would not teach that Islam is an inferior religion. I would teach the opposite of these things as passionately as I could. I would support the preservation of traditional African religious practices wherever I could and learn from them as I was able.

In no way am I denying the material and spiritual harm that colonialism and white missionary work have done to the African continent in myriad ways, particularly through the exploitation of natural resources and the repression of Indigenous culture. And yet, I recognize that my parents forged genuine friendships with Zambian people, some of which have endured for almost half a century. My father used his farming and carpentry skills, the ones he gained on his father's farm in rural North Carolina, to build infrastructure and agricultural resources in some of the most remote parts of Zambia. He worked diligently to train local pastors, so that they no longer depended on white missionaries to lead churches. I find myself ill-equipped to sort neatly the good from the bad. I presume only the Zambian people can determine this for themselves.

But I do think about reparations. I think about all that Zambia has given to me and how I can repay such generosity. As a form of spiritual reparations, I have dedicated myself to the practice of true interfaith dialogue, where the purpose is not to convert but to learn. This learning is both for the sake of helping me to understand others and honor their practices and also for the sake of helping me to broaden my own spiritual life. It is about learning to live peacefully in a pluralistic world and also about knowing the Divine more fully. It is about recognizing the limitations of my own faith tradition, as well as its gifts.

As a form of material reparations, I spend a lot of time strategizing about how to redistribute wealth back to Africa. Investing in the economic development of the Continent, no spiritual or capitalistic strings attached, would be one way for white American Christians to atone for our complicity in the colonialist-imperialist projects of the twentieth century. We owe a debt to Africa that Jesus cannot repay for us.

What's more---Africa is not impotent; she will form you and shape you, too. Perhaps the greatest paradox of my Zambian upbringing is that it taught me a counter-narrative to the myth of white Christian supremacy. It taught me that the world is full of people who are different from me in every possible way, and from the very beginning I understood that this is the way God intended. The blending of cultures, skin colors, foods, music, and geography that characterized my early childhood remain the default setting for me, so much so that when I find myself in a homogenized environment where the people are too much the same, my spirit cannot settle. As a child, I was not aware of any conversion project, only that it was right and good that everyone was not like me.

It turns out that even David Livingstone was a pretty awful missionary. He apparently converted only one African, who eventually gave up on the faith because he did not want to practice monogamy. Livingstone was a better explorer and physician and abolitionist, although the places he "discovered" were of course not new to the Africans who lived there. It is said that his written eyewitness accounts of the horrors of the slave trade contributed to the end of the trade in Africa, something of which he must have been proud. On the other hand, his expeditions into the heart of the Continent certainly opened up Africa to imperial conquest, though he himself was not an imperialist. From the perspective of many Africans, Livingstone's legacy, like that of the whole missionary enterprise, is complicated at best. It brings together in stark relief the range of human motivations---freedom and conquest, discovery and domination, altruism and ego, compassion and alienation.

And the farm house? These days the missionaries are gone, and the home is managed by local Zambians, who offer its storied rooms as a guesthouse for weary world travelers. A World House indeed.

Chapter 23

Risking Arrest

Although I had been pretty active with the Poor People's Campaign in Texas, prior to that meeting in the Spring of 2018, I had not planned on getting arrested. I didn't want to do it for the wrong reasons. I didn't want to do it simply because it is a little dangerous---I do have that side. I didn't want to do it to score points with fellow activists. I didn't even want to do it as a rite of passage aimed at amplifying my credibility as a progressive minister. In my corner of the Church world, getting arrested for protesting social injustice can be a resume-builder. This is, of course, a very different corner of the Church world than the one that is unwaveringly devoted to "law and order." But I didn't want to do it as a rite of passage or a resume-builder or any reason mostly about me.

My husband Jonathan and I had talked it over. We had married in 2013 and had our first child at the very end of 2014. Getting arrested could mean a night in jail; how would we explain that to our preschooler? Jonathan could handle it, but he would worry, really worry.

I went to the civil disobedience training that afternoon,

thinking I would engage in the protest right up until the point when police officers warned us to back away or be arrested. Then I would move and retreat into the safety of the crowd. Those gathered at the training sat around tables arranged in a large rectangle, inside one of the meeting rooms at a local union headquarters. We were a small, but diverse crowd---racially, religiously, in terms of gender, orientation, and age. I was the only clergy person in the room.

It was a Sunday afternoon, and I wandered in a few minutes late from Sunday morning preacher obligations. We were planning a demonstration for the following day at the Texas Railroad Commission Building. The Texas Railroad Commission, you should know, has very little to do with railroads; it's a convenient misnomer that helps conceal the failures of this institution. It is supposed to be at work enforcing safety and environmental protection standards across the state, which inevitably puts the Commission in a position to stand up to Texas' powerful oil & gas industry. Except that the commissioners are often elected with the help and support of substantial donations from oil and gas, presenting a clear conflict of interests. The Commission's failure to enforce environmental protections has resulted in death and disease in various places and circumstances around the state. And as is so predictably the case, the populations most affected by this lack of oversight are poor or people of color or low income people of color.

We munched on carrot sticks and sipped carbonated water, while listening to our lead organizers outline the protest logistics—how and where the march would begin, how we would gather as a large group in the lobby of the Railroad Commission to chant and sing and make our demands, how eventually a smaller group would make their way to the doors at the main entryway and plant their feet firmly in front, locking arms to block any entry into or exit from the building. It would be a peaceful but calculated disruption to business as usual, a civil form of disobedience.

Next, the local Austin lawyer who had volunteered to support the Poor People's Campaign through pro bono legal advice and representation explained what it would mean to be arrested---how the process would work from handcuffing to booking to release to appearing in court to paying fines. We discussed the potential risks and consequences for people who couldn't afford to miss work for a night in jail, for people who couldn't afford another arrest on their record, for people who worked for the State and couldn't afford an arrest at all. We all assessed our own levels of risk.

I began to notice how much privilege I had brought into that room, how much privilege I carry into every room. I had no previous arrest record at all. I direct a religious non-profit where I essentially supervise myself, so I knew my boss wouldn't fire me. I might even hear a "job well done" from our Board of Directors and members of the congregation.

I'm also a white woman, and the truth is that in this country, even disruptive white women are more likely to be seen as victims in need of protection, or misguided but harmless annoyances, rather than actual threats to public order. This is both a blessing and a curse. No, that's not quite right. What I mean to say is that in that moment, it was a clear advantage. Were I to be arrested, I imagined that my rights would be protected and that law enforcement would treat me with respect. I assumed that I would not be abused or die in custody. Like the way Sandra Bland died in a jail cell in Waller County. Or the thousands of migrants detained in prisons and concentration camps at our southern border. From these fates my whiteness would protect me.

On the other hand, I might not be taken seriously at all. I

am a woman. And young-ish. Even Whiteness cannot protect me from that.

What finally changed my mind that day about risking arrest was a single sentence I heard the Rev. Dr. Martin Luther King, Jr. say in his final speech, "I've Been to the Mountaintop," which he gave on April 3, 1968, the night before he was assassinated. He told the community that had gathered to hear him speak that they needed to be at the march the next morning, even if it meant leaving work or missing school. *Leaving work or missing school---* that was the line. I don't ever remember standing in a pulpit, asking a congregation to leave work or school, for any reason. Of course, Dr. King had the moral authority to ask this of people, having logged at least 30 arrests by the time of his death and all kinds of direct actions for the cause of civil rights. But these were not all people of privilege with flexible schedules and plenty of paid vacation. He was asking people to pay a price for something larger than themselves. And I felt that he was asking the same of me in this re-incarnation of the Poor People's Campaign that Dr. King and his co-conspirators had originally begun in 1968.

∽

While the seven of us were sitting there, blocking the entrance to the Texas Railroad Commission, we were given a first warning to move. Almost instantly, our leader Josh began singing, "We shall not be moved." It was a brilliant, even comical act of resistance.

Then a bizarre thing happened: After we had been warned a second time that we would be arrested if we failed to move, one of the cops approached me to try to talk me out of it. I don't know if it was my white collar or my white skin or my womanhood, but for some reason, he approached me and no one else, though clearly I was not the leader. He said, "You don't wanna do this. If you get arrested, it's gonna be all about you; it'll be a distraction from the protest. You don't want it to be all about you."

To his face, I smiled and nodded, "Thank you, Officer. I understand." There was something about his words that felt patronizing and paternalistic...as if I hadn't thought this through.

But the day before, I had already had this argument with the voice inside, "It IS about me, Officer. It is about ME deciding that if anything is worth going to jail for, surely it is the life-and-death issues we are addressing here today. And it is about the other 6 people beside me, making the same choice. And the 40 other people filling this lobby. And all those who may be inspired to act in their own ways, based on our actions here today."

These issues are worth at least 24 hours of disruption in my own life, even if the only thing that changes is my own level of commitment to the work of the Gospel. Even if the only thing that gets free is me---freer from my fear." Because freer people are kinder, more generous people, less prone to abuse or exploit their fellow humans.

I was keenly aware that my lone arrest was not going to end poverty and ecological devastation in Texas. Nor would the arrests of the other six souls I was with. Nor would the 1,000s of arrests that had occurred since mid-May around the country in connection with the Poor People's Campaign. But you know what can over time?

What can change the world is people who are willing to disrupt their normal routines and take on a level of personal sacrifice in order to resist what is wrong in the world.

What can also change the world is people who are willing to pay attention to the disruption, as if their attention is itself a holy and living sacrifice.

What can change the world is religious folks who are willing to engage protest as spiritual practice.

It turns out that it's pretty hard to get jailed for civil disobedience in Austin. This, ostensibly, is because law enforcement agents and judges lean more to the left in Austin, as opposed to the rest of Texas, and therefore give more leeway to public protest. I can buy that. I imagine it also helps if you're white. I say this because just last Spring, during the Texas legislative session of 2023, my friend and fellow activist was brutally tackled by four officers and taken to jail for far less than what I had done. Adri barely tops out at five feet tall, but they're spirit looms large. They have a fierce commitment to justice, yet one that is rooted in the warmest, deepest, gentlest of souls. Adri is also trans, nonbinary, and Latinx and was well-known for their powerful advocacy for the trans community, especially in the face of so much anti-trans legislation during that session. One afternoon, as Capitol police cleared the chamber of spectators during a particularly tense period of debate, Adri was attempting to usher their own constituency down the stairs and out of the building. In one of the most stark instances of targeting I have ever seen, four officers wrestled Adri to the floor and held them there under their weight while countless others walked past, unbothered. Adri, terrorized and traumatized, spent the night in jail. It sent a clear message of intimidation to both people of color and to transgender folx. In the end, the charges were dropped, but Adri no longer lives in Texas, another casualty of the state GOP's politics of hate.

On the day of my arrest, the officers said it just wasn't worth the time and effort and cost to take us down to jail. Instead they handcuffed us, detained us for a short while in a back room, and ultimately issued criminal trespass warnings to all seven of us. The trespass warnings barred us from returning to the TRC Building for a year for any reason without a special invitation.

As my new friends and I walked out the doors we had just been blocking less than an hour before, an African-American man, probably in his 30s, approached me and shook my hand.

"Thank you for what you did in there," he said. "I was the one standing nearby to your left when that officer was talking to you. I hope you didn't mind. I just wanted to make sure nothing went wrong." I had not really seen him before, but when he said this, my mind finally registered that he had been standing there all along.

"Oh, well, then I should be thanking you!" I replied.

"I wish I could have been blocking those doors with you," he went on. "But I'm on probation, and I just can't afford to be arrested again."

"Of course, I totally understand. I'm glad to be in solidarity with you."

This brief exchange confirmed that I had made a good choice, that it had been my turn. It also confirmed the deep paradox inherent in any activist and advocacy work: The work cannot be about me, but it has to be enough about me that I can identify what *my* role needs to be. Not because the world needs anymore white saviors; to be sure, Whiteness is one of the things from which we most need to be saved, so it cannot be about assuaging white guilt or being a "good white person." It can't even be about my own moral development or virtue, not at its core.

It has to be about the recognition that my liberation is tied up with everyone else's, and that, however precarious for them, everyone else's liberation is tied up with mine. We are in this mess together, for better or worse. In this framework, the practice of assessing my own level of privilege is not primarily a psychological evaluation, rather it is a very practical way of identifying what resources I have to offer on a particular day in a particular context. From this perspective, getting arrested was my offering to the community, not a personal achievement or a heroic act, however tempting it might be to pat myself on the back for being so woke or benevolent.

In that sense, it's *not* about me, just like every conversation about racism is not about something I've personally done wrong. But if conversations about racism or militarism or poverty or environmental devastation are never about me and my personal choices, chances are I am living in a deep state of denial. Somehow folks, like me, with a lot of privilege have to get better at taking responsibility without making it all about us.

Chapter 24

Behold, a Son!

I was pregnant the day I got arrested. Only a few days along, too early to be detected by a +/- on a stick, but I was pretty sure I knew when I left the Texas Railroad Commission, feeling dehydrated and just a little off. The odd and unintentional alignment of these life-altering events was top of mind when I called the birthing center to find out the sex of the baby"Do you have a feeling about what it is?" the nurse asked.

"No, not really. With my first child, I did. We were pretty sure it was a girl. And she was."

"Are you sure? A lot of women feel like they know?"

"I mean, maybe. But I'm not sure enough to say it out loud."

(Inner monologue: Well, I think it might be a girl. But I think that might be because I want it to be a girl. We have a really great name for a girl! But I've also been itchy. They say you can be itchy with a boy, on account of the testosterone. And so hungry. I've been so hungry. They say you can be more hungry with a boy ... .For God's sake, tell me what it is already!)

"Do you want me to tell you? Are you ready?"

"Yes. I'm ready."

"Congratulations! It's a boy!"

(Oh, no.)

"Oh, no" was my first thought. I'm sure that's not what I said to the nurse on the phone, but when I hung up, that's the distinct feeling that lingered.

I felt like God was trolling me, sitting on a high perch somewhere and laughing while I tried to metabolize this new information.

"All this time" giggles the Divine, "you've been calling yourself a feminist and going on about how we need a new kind of masculinity. Well, here you go: A baby boy so you can build a new masculinity from scratch!" At this point Mama God is flat out rolling on the floor cackling.

It's not that God is not a feminist; I'm sure they are. They just have a wicked sense of humor and irony, and apparently it will be hilarious for them to watch me raise a boy. All kinds of hijinks will inevitably ensue, I'm sure.

That is the central animating question that was plaguing me on the day my growing child's DNA data was revealed: How in the heck do I raise a boy in this society, especially a white one, without allowing his identity to be co-opted by toxic expectations that he will be aggressive, domineering, unemotional, entitled, and distortedly strong?

We decided that this boy-child's middle name would be Ruben, partly an homage to my mother Ruby and partly because it derives from the Hebrew for "behold, a son!" His gender reveal certainly felt like an epiphany of biblical proportions. Of course, we wouldn't know his actual gender until years later. Experts say that young children don't really perceive gender as a category until around ages 3-4, and it takes them a year or two longer to identify the gender that most closely represents them. What the nurse told us is that this emerging human would have a penis and XY chromosomes, and in our society, that meant folks were already layering him with ideas about who and how he should be.

There were the comments about how much more "active" he would be. Nevermind that his older sister was, relatively speaking, more rambunctious and physically vigorous than many of the other girls *and* boys in her preschool class. I think the jury is still out on which child of mine will be more "active." Or assertive/aggressive. Or emotionally expressive. But maybe it's not a competition, right?

On the level of meta-narrative, I keep thinking about how my boy-child was arrested...en utero. How his earliest days began with assessments of his mother's level of power and privilege, and by extension his. I keep thinking about Mary, the mother of Jesus, and the anthem she sang in preparation for her own boy-child.

"He has brought down the powerful from their thrones,
and lifted up the lowly;
he has filled the hungry with good things,
and sent the rich away empty."
(From the Gospel According to Luke 1:52-53)

Mary's Magnificat, as it is called, is a song of resistance to the political and religious status quo. It is all about the redistribution of power---out of the hands of those who hoard and oppress and into the hands of those they marginalize and exploit. It is about how God will use the birth of Jesus, Mary's son, to set things right.

In the Christian tradition, we have tended to obsess about the waters of baptism and the blood shed on the cross---these are the things that will save us, they say. But I think Mary's womb was just as pregnant---pun intended---with the possibility of salvation.

Don't get me wrong: I wasn't planning on birthing a Messiah. But isn't every newborn child a chance to start over? To make the world, at least your own corner of it, new and right again? I think this is a far superior theological framework than the one that says someone has to die in order for the rest of us to live. Why can't a birth remind us that transformation, *new* birth, remains a possibility for us all?

In this way, it IS about the water and the blood. The blood pulsing in my umbilical cord. The sweat and tears that labor will inevitably bring. The waters that will break, signaling new life on its way.

Chapter 25

7 Centimeters

There were moments of breathy mindfulness. And intervals of peaceful rest.

There were vulnerable tears of frustration and overwhelm and anger.

And there was the primal scream, a railing against the intensity of the pain. This is not what they recommend in birthing class. Breathe into the pain, they say. Don't run away from it, they say. Surrender TO it, they say. If you need to vocalize, they tell you to groan from the deepest parts of your register. And it is sound advice.

But for me, as contractions came stronger and faster, I felt compelled to cry out. The resistant rage of a higher note was necessary, a harnessing of the energy and power needed to survive the tidal waves of pain. I had to be angry at the pain before I could manage it, to be indignant before I could surrender.

The labor for my second child proceeded much as the labor for my first. I arrived at the birthing center with my cervix dilated to approximately 2-3 cm. Contractions were coming approximately five minutes apart and gaining intensity. The midwives and birthing assistants met Jonathan and me at the center just after 2:00 am on Wednesday, February 27. I had been experiencing mild contractions and lower back pain since about 5:00 pm on the 26th, but I had been able to make dinner and help put Vivienne to bed. Then I had tried to sleep, until my womb kept rousing me.

By mid-morning my cervix had dilated to 7 cm. But shortly thereafter the contractions slowed, and momentum stalled. This development gave me a bit of rest and a chance to gather my wits, but the reprieve also meant that things were not progressing.

"The same thing happened during my labor with Vivienne," I remarked casually to Meg, the midwife in charge. "I got stuck at 7 cm."

"Maybe you are afraid of going deeper into labor, where things get harder and more painful," she said directly and without irony.

I was livid. The nerve of her, suggesting that I had some sort of mental block or that I wasn't up to the challenge of a natural birth. I interpreted her assessment as criticism, as if she had flat out called me weak.

Truth be told, I wasn't sure I could do it---this all-consuming task of delivering a life, while feeling every harrowing sensation in your body, not knowing how long it will last, or even for certain if it will end well. And doing it all with nothing to dull the pain, not even a drop of something just to take the edge off.

"Let's try this," Meg said, carrying in what looked to be an oversized inflatable version of The Planters Peanut mascot

(™), that dapper yellow-shelled gentlemen in tophat and monocle. Indeed, the midwives refer whimsically to this tool of their trade as "the peanut," but it will forever be known to *me* as "The Peanut of Perdition." I can think of no better punishment in Hell (if I believed in such a literal place) than perpetual labor on the peanut.

"I feel mad at you," I declared, matching her candor.

"Good," said Meg, "Tell me about it."

"I am doing the best I can, but this back pain is killing me," I stammered back at her, through tears. "The contractions in my pelvis seem manageable, but the ones in my back are killing me."

I don't remember her exact words in response, but I finally heard Meg saying what I most needed to hear:

I see that you are suffering.
I also see that you are strong.
I am here with you.
And I will help you through it.

What if the central question posed by a natural birthing experience is this: *Can you be fully present to your life, in all its beauty and its mess? Can you do life without an epidural, even when it gets harder and more painful?*

The answer to this question might very reasonably be no. I chose the epidural with my first child, and I do not regret it. In labor and in life, there are times when the pain is just too much to bear, and numbing is what keeps us moving forward. But there are other moments when each of us can rise to the occasion and meet our lives head on, no filter and no drugs. In these moments it makes all the difference who is in the room with you.

I've learned in recent years that Black women are three to

four times more likely to die from pregnancy-related causes than white women. How can this be? Well, there are a variety of reasons, but one of them is that medical professionals often do not believe Black women when they say they are in pain. Tropes about Black women having higher pain thresholds somehow persist through medical school, prejudicing doctors and nurses, and leading to inadequate care. Disparities in access to pre- and post-natal healthcare to begin with only add to the crisis.

There is a terrible tension in this data. So often in our culture of white supremacy, white women are protected from the pain that could actually heal and teach us. Outside of Labor & Delivery, our comfort is prioritized not only to the detriment of people of color, but also to the detriment of ourselves and our children. For black women and other women of color, both in labor and in the world outside, their pain is not taken seriously enough. It is either thoroughly denied or effectively minimized to the point that it threatens their very survival, and the survival of their children.

∼

Meg returned shortly with a homeopathic remedy designed to help shift the contractions away from my lower back and more toward my pelvis. She also brought a dose of compassion. She was not letting me off the hook, but she had given me space for my anger to transform into energy.

I climbed back onto the bed, and Meg positioned that damned peanut between my thighs, strategically positioning my hips and legs so as to spark a new wave of contractions.

"We need them to come harder and faster now," she explained. "When the first one hits, you're going to want to fly off this bed and head for the door. Don't do it. I need you to stay here and breathe."

~

First the bloody show.
    Then the breaking of waters.
    As we pushed past 7 cm,
    my body fell into a rhythmic cycle---
    I would ride the wave of a contraction,
    Then I would vomit,
    Then the water and blood would flow from my pelvis.
    A little more each time. With each surge,
    more water, more blood.
    More blood, more water.
    With one final push, George Ruben Zercher was born at 2:35 pm. He was pink and healthy, with a dimple in his right cheek, just like his father's.
    The birthing assistant who attended George's delivery was Zambian.
    Did you hear that? The woman I quite literally leaned on as my body quaked during the most powerful surges of labor is Zambian. I had not met her before the birth, and I don't really know what this means. Except that it reminds me once again of how Zambia gave birth to me and now stands watch as I give birth to new kinds of life, working her spiritual midwifery on my soul.

Chapter 26

Foothills & Copper Belts: Mining for Kinship

"It was as if because of the very strangeness of my heritage, and the worlds I straddled, I was from everywhere and nowhere at once, unsure of where I belonged."
~Barack Obama, A Promised Land

"You are only free when you realize you belong no place. You belong every place, no place at all. The price is high; the reward is great."
~Maya Angelou

There is an African proverb that says those who are born on African soil are destined to be buried there. I have not tested the reliability of this saying, but it has been my experience that Zambians tend to grant unmerited honorary status to people born on their land, as if Zambia gives birth to you, as well as your human mother.

During my trip to Justo Mwale Seminary back in 2007, I had met Chewe. Chewe is also from the region of Zambia known as the Copper Belt, where Kalulushi, Kitwe, and

Serenje---the main towns I knew as a child---are located. Chewe belongs to the Bemba tribe, the tribe my father had worked with. When I first met Chewe, I told him I was born in Kalulushi, and he immediately and joyfully exclaimed, "My Bemba cousin!"

This is Zambian hospitality at its best, extending welcome with extravagance, naming you as family, as "one of us," with very little vetting process. In my case, knowing I came from the Copper Belt was kinship enough.

Who are my people? Which ancestry shall I claim?

These are complicated questions for me. My father's side of the family hails from the foothills of the Blue Ridge Mountains in western North Carolina, specifically the tiny town of Valdese. There is both French and German heritage on that side, and Fulbrights once were Volperts on the other side of the Atlantic. My mother's people hail from eastern North Carolina and once roamed the British Isles. I have strong Welsh and possibly Irish ancestry on her side.

When my family moved back to the US from the Copper Belt, itself a liminal space, we settled in the North Carolina foothills. The foothills are exactly as they sound, situated at the base of the Appalachians, rolling hills that gradually unfold into the Piedmont region of central North Carolina, until the landscape finally flattens out onto the Atlantic coastline.

When we moved to the foothills, I was homesick for Zambia. As a form of self-soothing, I had imagined that the foothills might feel like going home. After all, my daddy's people were from around there. I learned quickly that, to the locals, having relatives from a few counties over did not make you "from around here." And I remember riding in the car with my mother shortly after we moved, as she gently admonished my brother and me, "Now I don't want y'all to start talking like these people around here!" That was not the language of belonging. And confusing, too, because my mother's eastern North Carolina relatives speak their own variation on the Southern drawl.

The point is that I exist at the edges. This is a common experience of Third Culture Kids (TCKs), and it is true for me in multiple ways. I exist at the edge of my family, my culture, my nation, and my religious denomination. Just recently I found out that even my brain dances on the edges of what is neurotypical. As a neurodiverse person, even my neural pathways diverge from the mainstream.

I have a North Carolina cousin who used to play in a bluegrass band called "The Ward's Gap Pea-pickers." The twang of a banjo and a lonesome ballad resonate deep in my soul, but even bluegrass music is a kind of liminal sound. It is the folk music of the British Isles and southern evangelical revival songs blended with banjo and other forms of African percussion. Like me, it exists at the edges, where cultures and races rubbed together in poor and working class rural communities across the South, creating something new out of the friction.

Although I do not descend from a family of miners (moonshiners is more like it), the foothills and mountains of Appalachia are mine country, not unlike the Copper Belt of Zambia. Mines themselves are passageways between the pulsing energy of the Earth's core and the activity of life on its surface. There is a volatility at both the center and the surface that makes this liminal space precarious, even explosive, rendering those who wander it uniquely vulnerable.

Both Appalachia and the Copper Belt have known their share of exploitation and marginalization. There are missing mountaintops in West Virginia and generations of black lung disease because of the coal mining industry, not to mention poverty and drug addiction as fortunes have failed. What a poor inheritance for a region of the US that has powered much of the rest of the country for decades! In Zambia, British colonial exploits in the 1800s and now Chinese business expansion in the 2000s have extracted treasures from the African earth without proper care or compensation.

It occurs to me that those whose lives unfold in foothills and copper mines might become especially suspicious of outsiders. What I don't understand is why folks in the foothills of North Carolina and the mining region of Zambia have such different ideas about who actually belongs, because it turns out that those clans in the hills of North Carolina are more tribal than their rural Zambian counterparts.

I say I don't understand, but when I search my soul about it, I know that it's the Whiteness, at least in part. Whiteness depends on the dynamics of "othering," exploiting and amplifying difference in ways that make it scary or offensive, rather than beautiful and inviting. Ever since Bacon's rebellion in the seventeenth century, when the governor of Virginia, William Berkeley, put down the rebellion by turning poor Whites and poor Blacks against one another, wealthy elites in this country have been shoring up their own power by convincing poor and working class white folks that the only folks more powerless and unworthy than them are poor and working class people of color. (*Stamped*, Reynolds and Kendi, pp. 25-26). This dynamic has been playing out since before the American revolution, and certainly some of my people have bought this way of thinking 'hook, line, and sinker,' as they say. They are the ones now showing up at Trump rallies and wearing their MAGA hats to church.

There is that odd saying that "blood is thicker than water". I don't really buy it. There is much to be said for chosen family who embrace you in your fullness and with whom you are bound by a shared set of values. Even Jesus had chosen family. In the Gospel of Matthew Chapter 12, in a startling exchange, Jesus tells his disciples that "whoever does the will of my Father in heaven is my brother and sister and mother" (NRSV). Astonishingly, he says this *while* his biological mother and brothers are trying to get his attention over a large crowd. Not exactly a picture of traditional family values.

To my knowledge, I have not been disowned by any of my blood relatives, and yet I have not been claimed by many of them, either—not the unmasked version, anyway. Not the queer, feminist, neurospicy, preacher me. I am part of the family, I suppose, but I am not in the inner circle; I circumambulate the perimeter. Sometimes the view is clearer from here, and there is more freedom to move. Existing along the margins does not <u>*always*</u> mean being marginalized. It can be a gift to linger at the periphery of things. Sometimes you can see the good and the bad of a thing more clearly from that perspective than if you find yourself smack dab in the center. But the margins are lonely, too. I see that my siblings and I all have struggled with this dynamic in different ways, trying our best to fit into the contexts and communities in which we've found ourselves as adults. These contexts have been quite different--- my brother in working class rural North Carolina, my sister in a bit more affluent rural Alabama, and myself in the eclectic city life of Austin.

Of the three of us, I perceive that I am the one who has most tried to form an identity, however unconsciously, out of not quite fitting in. There is something about being like everyone else that has long felt confining and oppressive to me. But this too has its complications. What I have gained in freedom and authenticity does not cancel the sense of loneliness and disorientation.

What I am learning, though, after a lot of trial and error,

spiritual work, and therapy, is that belonging is not something that can be granted or earned; at the most basic and fundamental level of spiritual Truth, it just is. It turns out that the edges are still part of the whole. The center orients itself based upon the periphery. Margins give structure to the middle. Even people who live on the edge still do exist. And whether we experience it this way or not, we all belong to each other.

We often talk about needing to center marginalized voices. I do this myself. And yet I wonder if what is needed is simple acknowledgment and acceptance that the margins matter. That the perspective from the periphery is needed and that resources must be disseminated more widely so that they can reach as far as the outer edges of our cultures and communities, not always requiring people to migrate inward to thrive. Why not require those at the center to wander to the edge every now and again, past their gates and fences, across the limits of their comfort zones, just to listen. I mean *really* listen.

I, for one, want to be edgy and still belong.

Chapter 27

Seven Layer Shame Cake

[Self-reflection] If you have never survived a shame spiral so severe that you felt your soul might be in jeopardy, you may not be ready for this work.

In the fall of 2021, year two of the COVID-19 pandemic, I attended a writing workshop through the Collegeville Institute. I had so been looking forward to attending the weeklong workshop, which originally was set to be held at the St. Francis Retreat Center outside of Greensboro, North Carolina. I had anticipated the week as a time to give dedicated attention to writing this memoir; I had imagined that the literal return to North Carolina would parallel the emotional and spiritual journey I was making through my memories. in order to capture them and interpret them on the pages of my emerging book.

Because of COVID-19 the workshop was moved online. For me that meant Zooming through a day of the delicate and sometimes difficult conversations that can happen when you expose yourself in writing to strangers, and then shutting down my laptop in the evening to navigate dinner and bedtime routines with Jonathan and our two young kids. The workshop going online was one of the biggest disappointments of the pandemic. I had needed that time away so badly, and in the online format, I found it difficult to build the same kind of intimacy and trust that I had experienced at a previous Collegeville seminar.

I was already zoomed out the first day I logged in. I showed up mentally and physically worn out from the pressures of a new ministry job and a particularly difficult season of activism for reproductive rights in Texas. And also, I was just sad.

On top of all that, I had chosen to bring as my writing sample one of the previous chapters of this memoir, "The World House," in draft form, rough around some edges but ready enough for feedback and public consumption, or so I believed. I came tired *and sad*, and I also was nervous because this would be the first time I shared with anyone this writing about my heritage as a missionary kid and my grappling to come to terms with my family's participation in the legacy of white supremacy. My anxiety only increased when I realized that the seminar was comprised of six African-American women, four women with white skin like me, and three white-appearing men. I never had seriously talked about matters of race, European colonialism, and missionary work with so many Black people in such a direct and personal way. Sure, in seminary we talked about theoretical questions related to mission and evangelism, but we never talked about Whiteness and my family. I was excited about the possibility of genuine dialogue but also worried about how I might be received, the issues my writing would raise for everyone, and, to be perfectly frank, I feared that I might be rejected for the truth of who I am.

To make matters worse, the virtual format was a challenge for my neurodiversity. I am easily overstimulated during in-person meetings, and the computer screen saps my energy even more precipitously. Adding a further degree of difficulty, it is a side effect of old trauma that I enter new and unfamiliar territory needing to carefully assess the environment, looking for signs of danger, in search of guideposts that will guarantee my emotional safety and strategies for self-protection, should they become necessary. The experts call this hypervigilance. My senses scan the room, paying close attention to body language, noticing the energy of individual people and picking up on the collective vibe. In person I do this without thinking; it is my body's default setting. But it is almost impossible for my body to make these assessments about other bodies when they are not present in the room.

So I entered the Zoom room, feeling very untethered to anything secure, and tired, *and sad*. Then the imposter syndrome kicked in. Several of the participants came with PhDs. Not counting the facilitators, at least four in the group had published multiple books, and others had published either academic or spiritual writing. At this point in my personal writing trajectory, I had published several Op eds in Texas newspapers and a handful of sermons and short essays in a variety of online magazines and blogs. To be sure, a few of the folks came as true novices, but I still wondered if I deserved to be there. Perhaps paradoxically, in the same week that I attended this writing workshop, I also received an award for eight years of activism with the Texas Freedom Network. By external standards, I should have shown up confident and collected, but away from the spotlight of public recognition and accolades, my self worth was in shambles.

∽

On the third day of the workshop, it came time to present my writing sample. I gave some background about the book project, read the expected two-paragraph excerpt, and sat back to listen to the peer feedback. As with everyone else, we began with the affirmations—the things people appreciated about your writing, whether it be in the form, content, or style. As with others, my peers offered words of praise, naming what worked well and what resonated with them. So far, so good. Then one of the instructors prompted, "What questions do you have?"

The same person to speak up first in the affirmation stage immediately spoke up again. She seemed to be reaching for the right words. She even remarked openly, "I'm trying to figure out how to say this gently." In my hypervigilant heart and mind, this felt like a warning light. Is the critique so strong that she must find a softer vehicle for delivery? She seemed visibly annoyed. She was not yelling, but the tone of her voice was strained, somewhere between anger and exasperation. "You say that you haven't been able to confirm that the Bemba were matriarchal and matrilineal prior to the colonial period. Why not? *Why don't you know?* There's so much stuff out there these days. Have you not read any postcolonial theology? We even have postcolonial *feminist* theology now." Her voice trailed off in frustration.

I felt like I was sitting in an upper division undergraduate course, being berated by a professor for showing up unprepared. She was a professor in the academy, so perhaps this is not surprising, but it was not at all what I had anticipated. I had imagined comments about style or questions asking for clarification, perhaps advice about areas for expansion. I had even imagined that someone might challenge me to dig deeper on questions of race. Maybe even a suggestion of an author to read as a resource.

I couldn't quite tell if she thought I was ignorant or lazy, but it felt like I had offended something in her personally. Did she perceive me as just another White woman not willing to do her work? Did I perceive her as an angry Black woman? A few comments later, one of the facilitators of the group, herself also a Black woman, reframed this feedback as a question about whether my piece was pure memoir or whether I wanted to incorporate history and anthropology, turning it into something more like a personal essay. This suggestion echoed similar musings from my writing coach, and it came in a form I could metabolize more easily. But after the first criticism from the professor, something in me had already broken.

At first I just froze. Then I started to dissociate. I told myself to track the comments being made, in case there was something useful to hold onto for later. One part of my brain complied. Mental note. Mental note. I jotted a few key words and phrases on paper, while the rest of my brain powered down and went offline. Physically, I tried to brace myself as much as possible, so that I could keep tears at bay, at least temporarily, and so that I could resist the urge to disappear altogether.

After that first bit of critique, I tried to interject something about how I wanted my colleagues to feel free to comment honestly and not hold back for fear I couldn't take it. On the inside I was sinking, but I tried valiantly to stay afloat. Of course, I barely had begun to speak when one of the facilitators reminded me to hold my responses until everyone had given me their feedback.

So I sunk back into myself, trying simultaneously not to absorb too deeply the criticism that stung while also somehow remaining open and supple in the moment. Silence observed, the left side of my brain kept tracking. Mental note. Mental note. But the right side toggled between outrage and collapse, finding no stable footing.

"There's not very much of you in this chapter," said a colleague.

"Should missionaries even exist?" posed another.

I felt small and helpless and trapped, just as I had when I was a little girl, at the mercy of my father's rage, which also came on quickly and, many times, without sufficient warning. I remember a moment standing in the hallway of our home in Taylorsville, physically backed into a tight corner just outside my room, staring up into my parents' faces. My father is having one of his episodes. He has been yelling, and he grits his teeth, presumably to prevent himself from hitting me. I am sobbing, and he snarls, "Stop crying!!" Which of course I find impossible. I think I hear my mother mutter something in my defense. It is barely perceptible, but enough to distract him while I stumble backward into the safety of my bedroom and close the door.

The thing is that he never did hit me. But the threat of it was ever present, the specter of it always there. As a young girl of 8 or 10 or 12, I felt as if I were staring down a wolf, with teeth bared, ready to pounce at even the slightest misstep on my part. So I made myself as small and still and absorbent as I possibly could. Even the smallest whiff of defiance would send him over the edge.

∼

When all the feedback finally was given, I pulled myself together as best I could, trying to say something presently true in the midst of reliving old trauma. I had very little capacity to evaluate what had just transpired, except to know that it had felt unsafe, either because it was or because of what it had triggered in me. I did manage to answer for myself, and then I shut off my video and took shelter behind the silence of a dark

Zoom square. And I sobbed. And sobbed. And sobbed. The tears flowed unabated for a solid three hours, and then they seeped out sporadically as the evening drug on. It started as a spiral of paralyzing shame—that I wasn't enough, that my writing wasn't enough, that it had been foolhardy even to share it. Eventually the spiral of shame gave way to waves of grief and lament that crashed hard against the shore of my identity, steadily eroding the sand beneath me.

I felt like a seven layer shame cake in that moment. A comical culinary image, perhaps, for such a heavy layered burden. It reminds me, though, of the seven layer cake my friend's mother used to make from scratch when I was in high school. Seven thin layers of moist yellow cake and seven equally thin layers of chocolate icing, alternating carefully and neatly into one delicately unified creation. It was obvious to anyone who enjoyed a slice of this masterpiece that to bake it was a time-consuming endeavor, best attempted by someone with a lot of patience and an above average eye for detail.

And it was as delicious as it was beautiful, every bite the perfect ratio of icing to cake, cake to icing. Magnificent.

But unlike other two or three-layered cakes with thick bands of icing that can easily be scraped away with the proper utensils, unlike other cakes where the layers can be carefully separated out after assembly, this seven layer cake, once built, is a single organism nearly impossible to dissect or disassemble, like the layers of puff pastry or your very own skin. And you eat it and suddenly find that you've developed an aversion either to the flavor of the cake or to the icing, and you try desperately to separate them out and maybe ultimately just spit them out, because blech! What was once so satisfying is now so tainted.

This is me and my shame.

There is the layer underneath it all, something passed down for generations, I believe—a sense of fundamental not-enoughness that plagues my family line. This shame is the offspring of abuse, in some generations physical, in other generations, *only* emotional. ONLY, they say, because *they* can't see any scars.

There is the mental illness shame, passed down partly in the nature and partly in the nurture. I can name three people in my family origin that have diagnosed mental illnesses, and that includes me. But symptoms of depression, anxiety, obsessive-compulsive disorder, post-traumatic stress disorder, and addiction are readily apparent on both sides. The generational curses in my family are unresolved trauma and undiagnosed/untreated mental illness. I attribute my father's emotionally abusive episodes to unresolved trauma from his own childhood and untreated mental illness, and while experiencing mental illness can carry its own deep shame, the pressure or expectation to carry it in silence is debilitating.

There is the class shame, passed down mostly on my father's side, concealed as a kind of chip on the shoulder for proud country people. But underneath that pride is a sense of inadequacy that I carried through college and seminary and into my professional life. It has abated some as my earning power has risen, as I have ascended from a lower middle class upbringing to a solidly middle class adulthood, but it still lingers in corners, an added layer of emptiness at times.

There is the neurodiversity shame that I only recently have been able to name, but this too has surely been passed down in my DNA. HSP, ADHD and Autism Spectrum all have strong hereditary components, and I have some combination of the three. They are not diseases or deficiencies, but they can cause difficulties in a world designed for neurotypical nervous systems. The shame of noticing that you are not "wired" like everyone else, that you are more sensitive to stimuli than others, that you have trouble focusing or trouble shifting focus, that you can't process as quickly as others or sometimes you are processing everything at once, and not having anything to call this except a problem—this is the shame of undiagnosed neurodiversity. And even when you have a name for it, it takes work to reclaim this wiring as a gift.

It all is sandwiched together, and on top of it, in that awful moment in the writing seminar, here came the race shame. I don't think I have ever felt so White as I did on this day, confessing to a group of people, many of whom were Black, that I was a missionary kid. I was not used to that being a confession. In Southern Baptist circles growing up, missionaries were like minor celebrities. So it was not without suffering when, in that moment, this piece of my identity which had long elicited such pride, became the source of excruciating shame. I felt that they could see how fundamentally flawed I was, like they had perhaps seen it all along, like it was unsurprising to everyone but me. "The unbearable Whiteness of being" is what Dr. Chanequa Walker-Barnes calls it in her book, *I Bring the Voices of My People,* alluding to the philosopher-theologian Kierkegaard and his notion of the "unbearable lightness of being". Dr. Walker-Barnes was one of the facilitators of my workshop. She saw the unbearable Whiteness in me and my discomfort with my race being so central to the conversation.

I want to be clear that, in that moment, I was not ashamed OF my parents. I was ashamed FOR them, for all of us who in the name of "salvation" have tried to colonize the hearts and minds and homelands of people with our Whitewashed notions of God. When my colleague tossed that disembodied query at me, "Should missionaries even exist?" I clapped back, "This is not a theoretical question for me. Sure, I have a studied theological response to that, formed in a seminary classroom, but this is not a hypothetical question for me. If it turns out that my parents' life work was mostly a function of white supremacy, well, where does one go from there?"

This question terrified me at the time. With some distance and some healing, I can finally hold it without hyperventilating. It remains a central, animating question for me, and I have tried to weave some answers to it throughout the fabric of this book. It still gnaws at me, but I see that this question is not the last word about my life or my parents' legacy.

As I sat with my discomfort into the evening, the race shame gradually morphed into something more like grief and then eventually into a deep and wide lament for the vast inescapability of this problem of Whiteness. "Can 'white' people be saved?" I cried out to God in earnest. This was not some kind of melancholy self-flagellation, but a genuine recognition and an all-encompassing desperation about my condition as a person—on the one hand so "woke" and on the other so steeped, so marinated, so formed in White Western patriarchal Christian supremacy, that it might be impossible to outrun.

I have never cared much for the doctrine of 'original sin,' which suggests that all humans are born into sin, born fallen, like it's some kind of sexually transmitted disease. This doctrine is so often employed to shame people into 'believing' in God because they are fearful of burning in hell. It is used more casually simply to grind people into the ground by telling them that they are fundamentally broken.

But in that moment, I did feel originally sinful, like my only hope was a divine miracle. Like no matter how much I might read to educate myself, no matter how much I might dedicate myself to protest or policy change or reparations, I may never be free of the distortion of white supremacy. I guess this is what people mean when they say undoing Whiteness is a lifetime of work, plus some.

Thank God the Christian tradition has something better to offer us than original sin, and that is the notion that we are created good, that we are "fearfully and wonderfully" made (to quote the Psalmist). Not only are we good, we bear the imago Dei—the image of God—in our being. Yes, even white people. This is what makes it bearable, even possible to be white, but not White. The imago Dei in me may be pale as my Welsh ancestors in the dead of winter on the British Isles, but it is not a White person. This image within each of us, even a poor white sinner like me, is the "Grace that is greater than all our sin...".

~

This all was very tricky to sort through—the shame from the grief, despair from lament. Like a seven layer shame cake, I'm not sure it ever can be fully separated out. Maybe it doesn't have to be, but had I not been working on my mental health for twenty years at this point, through all kinds of therapy, had I not navigated terrifying spirals of shame on many previous occasions, I imagine I would not have had the inner resources or skills to name what was happening and reach out for help. To hold onto myself during the hours upon hours of uncontrollable tears, I texted with my writing coach, and she helped me find solid ground again.

Robin D'Angelo and others have written about the difficulty that white people often have in conversations about race in terms of 'white fragility'. White fragility accounts for why so many white folks become angry or defensive when people of color expound upon their experiences of racism. Alternatively, some white folks collapse into feelings of guilt, co-opting attention away from the painful experiences of the primary victims of racism. These defensive reactions are problematic indeed and inhibit progress in the work for racial justice, but I suspect that underneath so much of that fragility is shame.

I struggle with the word fragility because of the way it implies weakness. In the context of racial discourse, it is true that many White people have not developed the psychological strength and inner fortitude to have the hard conversations necessary. At the same time, people who deal with chronic shame, though they may be suffering from the insanity of racism, are almost inevitably strong and resilient people in many ways; they wouldn't be able to survive otherwise. The reality is that the people showing up with white fragility and the folks dealing with debilitating shame often are one and the same. In the writing seminar, it was me. If what underlies the shame is old trauma, then it almost certainly is a physiological response, not just an emotional one. These physiological responses can be reworked and reprogrammed, but it is a skill set that must be learned over time with awareness, gentleness, and self-compassion. You can't just get over it.

As I write about this experience, I hold some pessimism about our nation's capacity to address the crisis of systemic racism without also addressing the mental health crisis that plagues us at the same time. People with unresolved trauma have a lot of difficulty distinguishing what is truly dangerous from the false alarms. Anecdotally speaking, just within my own family, there seems to be a strong correlation between how much time someone has spent in therapy (or some other program of self-reflection and recovery) and their capacity to confront the truth about societal issues like racism and homophobia. Conversely, there seems to be a correlation between how much unresolved trauma a person has and their gullibility and willingness to be co opted by political conspiracy theories and cult-like religious fundamentalisms. Bessel van der Kolk writes about this susceptibility in *The Body Keeps the Score*, his bestselling book on trauma.

I am not saying that racism is a mental illness. There are plenty of people with mental health challenges who are people of color or who are white people doing their anti-racism work. I definitely am not saying that Black folks need to wait for all the White folks to go to therapy before they can have equal rights in this country. What I am saying is that the private, personal interior work makes the public, communal work of racial justice and reconciliation possible. Unlike many people of color, many white people have not needed to do our personal work as a matter of basic survival. We have not had to build resilience or hone coping mechanisms for managing the effects of systematic discrimination and daily microaggressions based on our race, as so many Black, Latine, Asian, and Indigenous people have. If you are a white man in particular, chances are that your social groups have often enabled your social and emotional dysfunction because challenging it could have been dangerous to the women, children, and racial minorities in the room. So many of us white folks have no practice at moving through shame and psychological discomfort in ways that open up healing, rather than rage and resentment. We need to practice.

To do anti-racism work, whether it is within our own psyches or out in our communities, necessarily involves disarming and dismantling our shame, alongside the ideology of white supremacy. It may seem counter-intuitive, but the only way I know to accomplish this is through naming the shame and making a steady commitment to self-compassion. It's the self-compassion that makes the discomfort of the shame bearable, so you can sit with it and breathe through it long enough to find out what it means, what it is trying to teach you, what new kind of life might be born if you can endure the

Amelia K. Fulbright

hard labor. Self-compassion is the midwife of transformation, the one who says,

I see that you are suffering.
I also see that you are strong.
I am here with you.
And I will help you through it.

Chapter 28

Why Don't You Know?

It took me over a year and a half, but when I finally was able to peel away the layers of shame cake and depersonalize the comments of my reviewer. When I finally was able to get beyond whatever barriers there were to our communication—the limitations of virtual technology, differing cultural expectations between white women and Black women about what constitutes constructive criticism and loving correction. When I finally was able to free myself from all the belittling voices in my head, I realized that my colleague had asked a powerful question, an important question, THE question: Why. Don't. You. Know?

I wonder, too, if what I heard in her voice was simply fatigue. Maybe she was tired of having to ask the questions that might startle well-meaning white people, like me, out of our ignorance. I wonder how many times a day, a week, a month, a year, she encounters a white person that just doesn't know what they don't know? And it is not benign ignorance, either. It is the kind of ignorance that, like the silence that is so often its accomplice, hurts people and keeps harmful systems in place.

1 *Why didn't I know that the Bemba tribe was once matrilineal and matriarchal?* Why do the typical Zambian histories only list notable colonial period political leaders or the lineage of male tribal chiefs?

2 *Why didn't I know that I could reject substitutionary atonement and still love Jesus, and still be Christian even?*

3 *Why didn't I know that it is not normal to live in fear of your father and emotionally unsafe in your own home?*

4 *Why didn't I know that it is okay to be gay?*

Why didn't I know...

"People have a right to information that affects them." This mantra was taught to all new trainees when I was hired to be an Advocate on the National Domestic Hotline in my first job after seminary. That was our job as advocates and crisis counselors on the hotline—to give callers the information that affected them. The phone number of their local domestic violence shelter, education on the dynamics of power & control in healthy versus unhealthy relationships, strategies for saving money on the downlow or avoiding physical violence until they could permanently leave the abusive relationship, the simple truth that "you do not deserve to be treated this way"--- all of this was information that affected them. It was never our practice to tell callers what to do, which only would have deprived them further of the power their abusers had been trying to steal from them, but we gave them the knowledge that could fuel their liberation. In this way, knowledge truly is power.

Returning to the question, "why didn't I know?" I suppose the answer is fairly obvious: It benefitted someone with power not to tell me, and it took repeated exposure to other worldviews for me to start asking questions.

Chapter 29

This Fragile White Woman's Tears

I CRY A LOT. I CRY WHEN I'M ANGRY. I CRY WHEN I'M scared or stressed. I cry when I'm overwhelmed and overstimulated. And yes, I even sometimes cry when I'm sad. For most of my life this has been perceived as weakness, liability, or emotional instability rather than healthy sensitivity. Whether it was my father shouting at me to stop crying, even as I was absorbing one of his tirades, or my former friend Shea remarking in judgment, "why do you always cry all the time," the signals were painfully clear—my crying was somehow an uncomfortable affront to them

So when I hear the words "white woman tears," I admit I find it hard not to hear them as a personal attack. Don't get me wrong—the instances in which white women have been known to derail conversations about racial injustice, to avoid personal accountability, and even to inflict physical harm on people of color with their tears and unfounded fears are real, common, and substantial. White women's actual tears have been some of the most lethal weapons of white supremacy, and I am not here to make excuses.

I think of the case of Amy Cooper, who in May of 2020 called the police to report feeling threatened by a Black man who had simply asked her to put her dog on a leash. Christian Cooper (no relation to Amy) was the African-American man there in Central Park, and he filmed Amy calling the cops. I cannot tell from the video whether she is shedding tears, but by the end of the call, you can hear the rising panic in Amy's voice. But panic about what? The presence of a Black man asking her to follow the rules?

Or worse, yet, the well-known case of Emmett Till, who was brutally murdered because Carolyn Bryant Donham thought he looked at her the wrong way. I don't know if Carolyn Donham actually cried on the stand, but it became clear that her temporary emotional discomfort was more important to the legal system than the life of a fourteen-year-old Black boy.

Or what about Kim Potter, the Minnesota police officer who shot Daunte Wright to death during a traffic stop? She cried on the stand, in a dramatic expression of remorse, using the defense that she only meant to tase Mr. Wright, not kill him. She was sentenced to only two years of prison for the killing. The judge in the case was widely criticized for such a lenient sentence. Even taking Potter's remorse into consideration, was Daunte Wright's life not worth more than a mere two years of penance? Over and over again in the US, the emotional comfort of white folks has been prioritized over the actual right of Black people and other racialized minorities to go on living.

At the same time I struggle with the language of "fragility" in general, whether we are talking about white fragility or male fragility, not because these aren't real phenomena, but because of the way the word itself is loaded with patriarchal assumptions about strength and weakness. Being fragile, delicate, and sensitive are stereotypically associated with femininity, or at least white femininity, and because women are stereotyped as the inferior, subordinate sex, anything fragile must necessarily be weak.

Not only is the word "fragile" so often associated with the feminine, it also carries negative connotations of disability. People who are especially emotionally sensitive might be viewed as "emotionally fragile". People with particular physical needs, limitations, or vulnerabilities might be understood as "medically fragile". Members of the disability community have long been trying to get the dominant ableist culture to understand that having needs, vulnerabilities, and sensitivities is not in itself weakness. It is part of being human to have needs and to rely on others in an interdependent web of existence. It is even okay to ask others to take special care around us when we are vulnerable. Similarly, women have long been trying to get the dominant misogynist culture to understand that emotions and intuitions are part of human being and knowing. Feeling and being will inevitably involve tears, and we need these salty ablutions to make us whole.

My tears often have functioned like an alarm system, alerting me that something in the environment is unsafe or that I am not being seen, heard, or understood. In childhood, I cried when I felt fearful of my father. In adulthood, I cry when I've been pushed to the limits of what I can bear—whether it is the demands at work, or the bodily pain of an illness, or when I am at my wits end emotionally. My tears are like the "check engine" light of my well-being. When they come, and especially when they come unexpectedly and profusely, I know it is time to take inventory, to take notice of whatever part of me I've been neglecting, and to take steps to give my interior life a tune-up.

A few years into my relationship with Jonathan, a funny thing started to happen. He is a funny man, and he makes me giggle daily. Occasionally, he or the children will cause me to laugh so deeply and fully that tears will come, the proverbial "laughed so hard until she cried." When these laugh-tears start to flow, I can feel the dam, the emotional barrier I've been erecting to shore up sadness, break and a hint of sorrow joins the current. My husband jokes that it's some kind of neurological problem and my kids take on a look of concern, but for me it is a form of catharsis.

So, yes, I *am* a fragile white woman. I carry my unconscious biases, and I sometimes don't know how to engage properly in conversations about race. I try my very best not to bring those manipulative white woman tears to any table where others are speaking hard truths. That's part of what so distressed me when my emotional dam broke back at the writing seminar, and I sobbed for hours. I cried with "video off" precisely because I did not want to derail the conversation. But on the inside, where old trauma is still reaching for relief, it felt like one more situation in which my tears were unwelcome, the old threatening voice demanding, "Stop crying!"

One of the challenges for people who manage mental illness or live on the spectrum of neurodiversity, or both in my case, is the challenge of emotional regulation. What we often are taught, either explicitly or implicitly, is to restrict or repress our emotions in order to behave in ways deemed more "appropriate" by the dominant culture. This restriction or repression is part of masking—what many neurodiverse people do to conceal their true thoughts, emotions, and physical reactions, in order to present themselves in ways that seem acceptable to more neurotypical folks. It strikes me that there is a point of intersection here between the way that neurodiverse people are pressured to mask and the way that Black women have for centuries carried the weight of being strong—always being the ones to work tirelessly, the ones who must stay positive and keep their families and faith communities encouraged, the ones who prop up our American democracy over and over again without proper recognition or compensation. White women are allowed the luxurious privilege of being helpless at times, or even just human enough to be alternately sad, joyful, angry, or annoyed. Black women, on the other hand, must only emote in ways that keep white folks comfortable. A similar pressure applies to neurodiverse folks. If you are neurodiverse and a person of color, I imagine the pressure only compounds.

Masking can be a helpful temporary strategy, but it mostly works to keep neurotypical people feeling comfortable and in control. It doesn't actually help neurodiverse folks learn how to honor, process, and eventually modulate their powerful emotions and physical sensations. Over a long period of time, neurodivergent people who mask may find it difficult to even identify their truest needs, desires, and feelings because they have been hiding and silencing them for so long.

So, yes, I *am* a fragile white woman. I am what people sometimes call "high functioning," but that's because my disabilities are mostly invisible, except to those closest to me. I have been managing depression, anxiety, and hypersensitivity since I was a child, even before I knew what names to call these things. Turns out I am so good at masking that it has taken me to my mid-40s to finally be evaluated for autism. As a person with a highly sensitive nervous system, I notice subtle changes in temperature, volume, the arrangement of objects, and movements, and I notice the very slightest changes in the energies of other people. I am both empathic and hypervigilant, and my finely tuned nervous system often keeps me safe. But when a person like me, who is sensing all the things all the time, sometimes just her own feelings but too often the emotions of others as well—it is no wonder the tears come so easily. Sometimes tears are the only thing I have to relieve the pressure.

Somewhat paradoxically, in my work as a pastor I'm often told that I have a peaceful presence. Some of this has been hard-earned through lots of practice, cultivating stillness in chaotic and emotionally volatile environments. Other times, I'm just really, *really* good at masking.

In *White Fragility*, Robin D'Angelo suggests that when a white woman finds herself in a cross-racial conversation and her tears begin to flow, that she take a few moments to assess what is at the root of these tears—guilt, shame, anger, empathy, embarrassment. If she is not able to contain her tears in a way that keeps her from derailing the conversation, D'Angelo recommends that she leave the room and take some time to process the emotions elsewhere. This strikes me as a healthy way to regulate and modulate emotions, provided that the person in question has some strategies to do this and some emotional support as needed. The layer I would add is this: For people with invisible disabilities, like autism, it may be more difficult to keep these emotions in check. And if a neurodiverse person participates in a cross-racial conversation inappropriately, once they recognize their mistake, the shame spiral that follows may be particularly brutal.

I reckon, to use a Southern word akin to a reckoning—that moment when we settle our accounts—

that we need to get to a place as a society where we shed our tears for healing,

for catharsis, for repentance and lament,

so that our tears mingle as medicines and not toxins.

In the final analysis, I know I want to live in a world

where Black women don't always have to be stoic just to survive,

and Black women can cry without having their strength questioned or denied.

I want to live in a world

where white women don't have to claim victimhood to earn the respect and solidarity of white men,

and a white woman can cry without causing someone to die.

I want to live in a world where boys and men can cry openly and without shame.

And I want to live in a neurodiverse world where sensitivity is understood as a gift to hone, not a defect to bury.

Anything short of this will keep depriving us all of our full humanity.

Chapter 30

Mosi-oa-tunya (The Falls)

Groundbreaking feminist theologian Mary Daly was known for saying that "if God is male, then the male is God." It follows that "if God is father, then the father is God." This maxim came true in my home, and it is why I am here in these pages, laboring both to dismantle the god-like hold my father has had over my wellbeing and to deconstruct the image of God as Father, as well. As we learn and grow, so do our conceptions of God grow and shift, too—or at least mine have

The classic Christian Trinity is this—God the Father, Christ the Son, and the Holy Spirit. Sometimes the Trinity is interpreted in contemporary terms as Creator, Redeemer, Sustainer. The former focuses on the "persons" of the traditional Trinity, and the latter describes their activity in the world. But these days my credo looks something like this:

God is Love.
God is a Black Woman.
God is The Falls.

It's a mish-mash of things: the nebulous notion of "love," a very particular kind of human body, and a natural wonder. I know some will think it sounds like heresy. So be it.

Let's start with the easy part: Surely God is love. This is the most precise description of divinity in the New Testament, in 1 John 4:16. Anywhere and everywhere that we find genuine love, we find the Divine. Sometimes it may look like a father, but very often it will not. Sometimes it may look like a mother, but very often it will not. Just as there are many kinds of quiet, and many kinds of silence, so too there are many kinds of love ~~~ queer and straight, platonic and romantic, parental and protective, healing and liberating. Love is not simple or singular; it is transcendent and yet deeply immanent at the same time.

Sometimes I do need God to be a person, because the bigness of Love is just beyond my grasp and too slippery to latch onto. Sometimes I need the God of Love to challenge as well as console me, and when I do, most often God is a Black woman. In her book of the same name, *God Is a Black Woman*, author and theologian Christena Cleveland describes the invitation extended by this kind of divine feminine:

> ...the Sacred Black Feminine welcomes us all with open arms. Unlike whitemalegod, She doesn't exclude anyone; Her circle is wide and all are welcome. But just because all are welcome doesn't mean all are ready. For though She is the Mother of all, She is especially the Mother of Black women. And though She is the protector of all, She is unapologetically Black and unapologetically concerned with the flourishing of Black women. Regardless of our racial identity, in order to experience the fullness of Her transformative love, we must get into formation around Her unapologetic Blackness. But we do not have to do this

> *healing work on our own. She Who is Unapologetically Black empowers us all beyond mere beliefs and into transformative action. She is Love-in-Action and She is simply waiting for us to say YES. (p. 219)*

I see God in the "Love-in-Action" of Black women who get out the vote when democracy is on the line and every election in between. I see God in the Black women who labor for reproductive justice and organize for gun violence reform. There are moments when the Sacred Black Feminine steps in to rescue us from danger, even when we haven't earned it and the mess is of our own making. But She is not a savior who will let us skate into eternity on a single sinner's prayer or somebody else's sacrifice. Ultimately, She makes us do the soul work and the self-work that will lead to redemption for ourselves and the world around us. One way or another, She will teach us how to love ourselves and each other. As the Apostle wrote in Philippians 2:12, She wants us to work on our own salvation, not for some afterlife but for an abundant life in the here and now.

I even see God in the Black woman who asked me that painful question, "Why don't you know?" Though it took me quite some time, now I see. Sometimes we do need correction, and in these moments, we are blessed that God puts us in our place. But this is not the shaming, punitive correction of whitemalegod, as Cleveland calls him. This is the creative, life-giving correction of the God who is Love and comes so often in the flesh, in my time and place, as a Black woman. And this kind of correction does not stop at negation; it always brings forth new life and helps us to find our place again. Our "place in the family of things," as Mary Oliver says. This is when God becomes The Falls.

Mosi-oa-Tunya—my favorite place on Earth

I tell people that my favorite place on Earth is Mosi-oa-Tunya, the local name for what the British would later call Victoria Falls. Mosi-oa-Tunya translates to "the smoke that thunders" in the Lozi and Kololo languages. The name points to the fact that you can see mist rising off the falls and hear their roar from literally miles away, like a drumbeat calling you home.

The last time I visited Mosi-oa-Tunya was in 2007, on the seminary trip I already recounted. I recall walking carefully along the edge of The Falls, where there is remarkably minimal railing. Wearing a powder blue raincoat and safari-style hat that was (regrettably) not at all waterproof, I paused to peer down into the depths at the Zambezi River in the canyon below. It can be dangerous to get so close to divinity. The Hebrew Bible warns against staring directly into the face of God, lest you lose your sight. Moses dared not approach the fiery bush all ablaze. God is always a little bit dangerous. But The Falls will take care of you, too. They ask for no profession of faith or confession of sin, only that you sit and stay a while, and allow these ancient waters to baptize you once again—body and soul.

There is something about The Falls that makes me feel small, but in the good way, not the bad. They remind me that I am a creature, not the Creator, and that this is a blessing not a curse. They bring me back to my body, which is the sacred vessel in which my spirit burns. Returning to bodies and our creatureliness can remind us of both our mortality and our animal selves, and so we often avoid dwelling on our creatureliness precisely for these reasons. But being a created one—sometimes strong and sometimes weak, yet always dependent on our Creator—is part of what it means to be fully human.

I love that line of Mary Oliver's poetry that says: *"Let the soft animal of your body love what it loves."* This, too, is a form of faith, of trust in God the Creator, and I feel this kind of love at The Falls. Beside those waters, I am a tree that trusts, and God is The Falls. For me the Spirit is in the water, always somehow in the water. From my baptism in the Mumbi to the waters of my womb to the rain that renews our Earth and makes her come alive again.

Love ~ Accountability ~ Creativity: This has become my Trinity. Love in all its forms ~ the Accountability of a Black Woman (and all who seek justice relentlessly) ~ and the creative sustenance of The Falls, in all the ways that water shows up in my life. Sometimes God is human and personal. Sometimes God is cosmic and universal. Sometimes they are Earthbound and organic. But they always ARE, and they always are available.

Chapter 31

Why I Am Writing This Now

"I think midlife is when the universe gently places her hands upon your shoulders, pulls you close, and whispers in your ear: I'm not screwing around. It's time. All of this pretending and performing – these coping mechanisms that you've developed to protect yourself from feeling inadequate and getting hurt – has to go. Your armor is preventing you from growing into your gifts....Time is growing short. There are unexplored adventures ahead of you. You can't live the rest of your life worried about what other people think. You were born worthy of love and belonging. Courage and daring are coursing through you. You were made to live and love with your whole heart. It's time to show up and be seen."
~Brené Brown

Maybe I'm having a midlife crisis, although according to Brené Brown, it's not a crisis. It's more like a reckoning. I set out to write this memoir of the "first half of my life" because I felt the need to understand the first forty-ish years, in order to know how to live in the second. I'm writing this because I can't keep plugging along the way I have been, telling half-truths about my childhood and protecting my father by being less than who I am. I need to say the quiet part out loud about my own traumas—the emotional abuse from my father, the alienation from my birthplace, the waking up to the ways that Whiteness has formed me, the ways that toxic religion made me ill. It's not just that there have been traumas, but that so many of these dynamics have been justified and sanctified with harmful theology. When God is understood as a Father and your own Father is abusive, you end up living in fear of both. That will make you sick over time, if not physically, at least spiritually and emotionally.

I'm writing this because I am in my mid-forties, and my forties have been hard years. My twenties were also hard years, the years of my most debilitating episodes of depression. Every time depression has shown up in my life it has been a sign that my coping mechanisms are no longer serving and, instead, are confining me. It's like my psyche's way of saying that it's time to level up or....die, either literally or emotionally and spiritually. It is my system's way of powering down because it can't keep functioning without a software update or a defragging of some kind.

Thanks to a decade of various combinations of therapy, meds, acupuncture, herbs, meditation, friendship, growth, spiritual direction, and ultimately divorce—my thirties gave way to some of my healthiest years. I graduated from seminary, married Jonathan, founded a ministry, and delivered my first child. I've been diligent with mental health maintenance, but my forties have brought new challenges—postpartum depression after the birth of my second child, a pandemic, political violence and chaos, a call in an unhealthy church system, hormonal changes. I have gone back on my meds for depression and anxiety, the same ones that rescued me in my twenties.

I feel some sense of defeat about this, as if somehow the trauma has won. But you can't outrun brain chemistry, and you can't outrun trauma, either. Some of the old traumas are showing up again. Here's the thing, though, that I see so clearly in midlife: The traumas aren't trying to win, but they are very much asking to be dealt with. They will not be minimized or dismissed or worked around. They are begging me to say the quiet part out loud, to tell the family secret, because the silence and the secrecy—the armor—are starting to suffocate me.

I haven't spoken to my older brother in over two years, after talking with him began to feel like talking to one of the strangers that sends me hate mail for affirming queer people or advocating for reproductive justice. My brother says that he loves me, but he doesn't really know me, and yet he really hates people like me. As I have drifted to the left of my parents over the years, politically and spiritually, my brother has drifted to the right. For many years, I was marginally conscious of this fact; I knew, for instance, that he had been a Rush Limbaugh devotee at one point. But it became tragically more clear during the Trump years. As with so many families, the Trump Train derailed whatever semblance of shared history and values had been holding family members together, however tenuously. My brother took his wife and kids to a Trump rally. Q-Anon conspiracies started popping up on their Facebook feeds. When I finally spoke up to my brother about how his support of Trump, about how Trump's alliance with the Christian Religious Right posed all kinds of dangers to so many people that I know and love—my queer and trans friends, my friends who are people of color, women in general, he responded only with defensiveness and more conspiracies. Except that he was also careful to mention that he still believes it's sinful to be gay, just to be sure I understood, even though I didn't ask.

That was when it dawned on me that it had been over ten

years since I had become an ordained member of the clergy, and not once in that decade had my brother ever asked me about my work. Not even a casual, "How's work?" I had always attributed this somewhat odd omission to busyness. My brother was raising small children. He was working. We lived far apart and neither of us are big phone-talkers. All true. But when the ties that bind were loosened (if not completely severed) by the MAGA movement, it occurred to me that perhaps my brother had never asked, even when we were together over holidays, because he didn't want to *know* about my work. Or worse—that he had some inkling of what my work is about and refused to acknowledge who I am and what I do.

This is painful, and it is no small thing because my work IS who I am. It is not all of who I am, but it *is* who I am. Advocating for the rights of LGBTQ2IA+ people is not just what I do, it is who I am because I *am* queer. Advocating for reproductive freedom and dignity, including access to abortion, is not just what I do, it is who I am because I *am* a woman who will fight for my own agency and bodily autonomy. I am a Christian pastor who rejects the distortion of Christian faith that my brother now accepts as orthodoxy—that is not just what I do, it IS who I am. If he had ever asked me about my work, the honest answer would have been that my work is to repair the damage done by people like him in the name of God. This is what is true, and it is painful. When my sister was lamenting (understandably) the breach between my brother and I, I remarked that I need my family to stop asking me to be in relationship with people who are harmful to me, even and especially when they're family.

That's the long and the short of it. I need to name the harm, and I need to stop being in relationship with people who are harmful to me. Because it *harms* me. It deprives me of energy and courage and joy. To keep going back into systems where I have to play small harms me, and in so doing, it robs me and my children and my spouse and my friends and my congregation of the best things I have to offer this world.

I don't know, yet, how I'm going to set all the boundaries or say all the things, but here in midlife, I am more than ever committed to being Amelia: Breaker of Silences, Breaker of Cycles. As the saying goes: If nothing changes, nothing changes.

The most difficult dilemma of these days is the same one that surfaced in the car in the conversation with my mother when I was in high school, except this time I am the one who wants a divorce. I am no longer angry at my father—that was the reckoning of my twenties. I am not living in resentment and unforgiveness. I just no longer have the energy or inclination to keep going back into any home where I have to play small. It makes me sick to do it, and I want to be well.

The dilemma, which has existed for decades, is this: When my mother made the decision to stay, from that day forward, I have been forced to choose between my own mental health and my relationship with her. My parents are still very much a package deal. Going back into their home is, for me, knowingly going into a toxic environment in order to maintain a relationship with my mother. I can choose to stay away and spare myself the exposure to my father, but if I stay away, my bond with my mother suffers its own dis-ease. It is a terrible choice. I am writing this because I want to have better choices. I want to stop making the choice to re-expose myself.

I am writing this now because I am so weary of the weight of being from a "perfect missionary family". This facade of perfection is the very thing that keeps us badly broken. But I worry that you, Dear Reader, will judge me for this, for wanting a divorce. I worry that you will say that I am not honoring my father and mother. I also worry that you will speak about me in hushed tones with the accusation, "How could she?! How could she air the dirty laundry on the front lawn this way?"

As bell hooks wrote in *The Will to Change: Men, Masculinity, and Love,* "Keeping males and females from telling the truth about what happens to them in families is one way patriarchal culture is maintained … .This silence promotes denial. And how can we organize to challenge and change a system that cannot be named?"

Reader, I am no longer comfortable with a silent unity that covers over pain. No, it's not that I'm not comfortable; it's that my body and spirit can no longer abide it. Secrets make us sick. Shattering the facade is the point. I no longer accept that it honors my father and my mother to keep quiet and pass down the trauma that has come to me through generations. I suspect that this trauma goes back, in some form, for generations on both my father *and* my mother's sides, perhaps as far back as ancestors I cannot name. My Grandpa Fulbright physically *and* emotionally abused his family, my father *only* emotionally abused ours. Somehow my dad figured out how to keep from hitting us with his fists, though he still bruised us with his words and ideas and expectations. It is a strange kind of progress. Yet from this perspective, we see that my father is not a singular villain; he is both victim and perpetrator. I believe it honors him, in the ultimate sense, to keep the generations moving toward deeper healing and greater wholeness, to break cycles of violence wherever I have power to do so.

I have this dream that one day I will be able to sit in a room with my father and the usual triggers of my trauma without being harmed. I have this fantasy that one day I will reach such a state of pure love and enlightenment that my own loving energy will envelope the room, that I will be able to sit in the space and not be overpowered by pain. That the power of my own healing will transform the space between us. But I'm not there yet. I'm not Jesus. I want to be like Jesus, but I'm not there yet. Maybe with time, meds, more therapy, more mindfulness, maybe some psychedelics, and spiritual discipline, I will get there. But I am reminded that before Jesus died on a cross. Before he rose again, overpowering both the authority of empire and the finality of death. Before he said, "Father, forgive them for they know not what they do." Before all of that, Jesus turned over tables in the Temple and announced that his true family were those that kept his commandments. Jesus did not suffer in silence or settle for half-truths. What would Jesus do? Resist, resist, resist all that deprives us of the healing and wholeness God desires for us. I can no longer preach this from a pulpit without claiming the truth of it for myself.

∽

I also am writing this now because I also want to be accountable for my own choices, my own mistakes, for the ways I have harmed others. Breaking the silences that have been forced upon us and bringing our stories into the light of day can dispel the shame they hold over us. At the same time, accountability is what breaks cycles—holding ourselves accountable and opening ourselves to others when they tell us the truth about ourselves.

Chapter 32

Upstream

"But let justice roll down like waters, and righteousness like an ever-flowing stream."
Amos 5:24 (NRSV)

WE NAMED OUR SECOND CHILD—THE ONE BIRTHED with the help of Midwife Meg, her peanut, and the Zambian attendant—George. For his great-great-uncle George on his Dad's mom's side of the family, the Musselmans. The one who worked as a sports journalist in Denver. He had a dark complexion and tight black curls, and people say he looked like Sammy Davis, Jr., often pointing to this as evidence that the Musselman line was a racially mixed one.

George. For George Orwell, British author and journalist perhaps best known for his novel *1984* about an authoritarian oligarchy, which at one time read like science fiction and now seems eerily prescient about the current state of US politics.

George. For George Harrison, guitarist for The Beatles who became known for his spiritual conversion and interest in Eastern religion and philosophy later in life.

George. From the ancient Greek for "worker of the soil" or farmer, more colloquially.

George for the mystics and truth-tellers and caretakers of the earth that the world will so desperately need to survive in his lifetime. Lovers and fighters who will not sell their souls for the temptations of late stage capitalism and the lies of the so-called "prosperity Gospel."

We named him George in February of 2019, and he changed our world. In May of 2020, another George---George Floyd---with ties to North Carolina (where much of my family lives), Houston (where my mother and father-in-law live), and Minnesota, changed the world for the better, yet in the worst way possible through the loss of his own life. George Floyd, as the reader may know, was murdered by a police officer in a particularly egregious, though not uncommon, occurrence of police brutality against a black life. As this George struggled to breathe under the knee of an oppressive policing system, rooted in over 400 years of slavery, segregation, and persistent anti-blackness, this George called out for his momma.

Many have remarked that when George Floyd cried out for his mother, his plea reverberated around the world and in every womb and maternal spirit. It is as if he was summoning Mother Earth herself, Goddess, Divine Feminine, Mary the Mother of God, and all the other earthly mothers who embody her sacred energy.

These days I ruminate on what my George, who was just beginning to form the syllables "Ma-ma" in May of 2020 has to do with this George, the one who mouthed them with his final breath. What I know is that I want to work for a world in which my George, a white child, and this George, who was himself a kid once, both can grow up being judged as Dr. King imagined, by the content of their character, not the color of their skin.

At first it occurs to me that the shaping of this kind of just and equitable world hinges heavily on our capacity to love other people's children. I am reminded of what my childhood friend Carrie once said about how my own mother treated her, "She loved me like one of her own."

We have to be able to love other people's children like they are our own, way before they are crying out in desperation from their asphalt death beds. We must love them in the voting booth, at City Council, and on the PTA. In the parks, and at preschool, and in clinics and courtrooms. One of the primary complaints I hear from Black mothers is that their children are not allowed the full innocence of childhood that so many fairer-skinned children are afforded. Black boys are criminalized, and Black girls are sexualized way. too. soon. Meanwhile, many white parents of means try to sequester our children (sometimes consciously, sometimes subconsciously) in affluent colonies of what we think is safety, under the banner of school choice or religious freedom or the free market economy. But if we want to love other people's children like they are our own, it is not going to be enough to invite them to our vacation bible schools and avoid them the rest of the year. Rather we must expend whatever political and social capital rests at our disposal to structure a world where education, healthcare, and economic opportunity are accessible and equitable for everyone. We must not be content to send other people's children to schools, clinics, or jobs where we would prefer our children never go.

So yes, we must love other people's children as our own, *and also we must disabuse our own white children of the myth of their innocence.* This, in fact, is the true "white man's burden"---to civilize our own children rather than to colonize everyone's else's. By civilize, in this case I mean to deprogram their white supremacist consciousness and replace it with identity that is rooted in a multi-racial, multi-religious, multicultural vision for their own communities and the world.

Along those lines, Dr. King's vision of a world where people are not judged by the color of their skin will not emerge as long as white folks attempt color-blindness. This may seem paradoxical, but the only way to undo white supremacy is to begin by perceiving it more clearly.

When my daughter Vivienne was about three years old, I picked her up from preschool one day and found her teacher on the verge of tears. The teacher pulled me gently aside and retold an incident that had occurred an hour or two before on the playground.

"Celia and Vivienne were inside the playhouse. Jalen wanted to join them, but they told her that this game was just for people with light skin. I think Celia is the one who said it, but Vivienne was part of it, too."

I could feel shame welling up behind my eyes as she spoke, and anxiety tying a knot in my abdomen.

She continued, "I gently redirected them and asked them to be kind and not exclude any of the friends. It was all I could do to keep from crying in front of them."

I was mortified. My mind began to race. *My child will not be a racist. My child will not be a racist. Is my child already racist? My child will not be a racist. Well, at least she is not the one who said it. Why would Celia say such a thing? Are her parents racist? My child will not be a racist. Maybe she should not play with Celia! Oh my God, poor Jalen. How awful for her? Is she okay? Maybe I should apologize to her mother. My child will not be a racist.*

Clearly, I panicked. We gathered up Vivienne's things as usual, and got in the car for our short drive home. I asked Vivienne about the incident. With the candor of a child, she described the sequence of events essentially in the same way her teacher had done, except in Vivienne's retelling it was a classic choosing of sides on the playground, of affiliating with one best friend by excluding another, wherein skin color became an easy way to distinguish and divide.

On the one hand, this is exactly what children do. As they grow and learn to navigate their environment, they also must learn to categorize and label. It is a way of getting a handle on things in a world that might otherwise be constantly overwhelming with its endless variety. Vivienne and Celia were not being kind, but they were not really being racist, either.

No. Stop. Rewind. In the context of over 400 years of systemic racism and anti-Blackness in our country, I struggle to imagine any comment about skin color, particularly one that excludes, that is *not* laden with the weight of bigotry. Our children see color; we all do. This in itself is not wrong; in fact, it is natural. As the parents of white children, what we must do is to help our children see not only color, but also *how color functions* past and present in a racialized society. We must make them fully conscious of what they see, so that they will not unconsciously perpetuate the lie of white supremacy.

That day on the playground was a turning point for me. I realized at that moment that I was behind. <u>Very behind.</u> This was confirmed not long ago when I read the following in an online article published by the American Psychological Association:

"In an online study with a nationally representative sample, more than 600 participants were asked the earliest age at which they would talk with children about race. They were also asked when they thought children first develop behaviors and cognitive abilities relating to race and other social factors. More than half of the participants were parents while 40% were people of color. The research was published online in the Journal of Experimental Psychology: General®.

The participants believed conversations about race should begin near a child's fifth birthday even though children begin to be aware of race when they are infants. Previous research has shown that 3-month-old babies prefer faces from certain racial groups, 9-month-olds use race to categorize faces, and 3-year-old children in the U.S. associate some racial groups with negative traits. By age 4, children in the U.S. associate whites with wealth and higher status, and race-based discrimination is already widespread when children start elementary school."

The moral of the story: Most parents (regardless of race) are waiting too late to talk with their children about race and racism. The title of the article: "Children Notice Race Several Years Before Adults Want To Talk About It." Indeed. As confirmed both by science and my own painful anecdotal evidence.

On the way home from preschool, I spoke sternly to Vivienne about how we must never disrespect or exclude someone because of their skin color. To the best of my ability, I spoke in developmentally appropriate ways about how Black people often have been mistreated in our country and how we must be careful not to repeat those mistakes. To be sure, the failure in this situation was more mine than Vivienne's, more ours, as in the collective White western "we", than mine alone.

Since that day we have added a whole array of children's books to our home library, books about the beauty of diverse skin colors. We've read and watched shows about key figures of the abolition and civil rights movements---Frederick Douglass, Harriet Tubman, Rosa Parks, and the Rev. Dr. Martin Luther King, Jr. We've even broached the subject of police brutality in the here and now. We work intentionally to expose her to people of diverse races and backgrounds. And yet, we have only just begun. *And we are still behind.*

The Water and the Blood, the Blood and the Water

∼

White supremacy is the water in which we swim. If you live in the US, regardless of skin color, you are automatically subscribed. There is no opting in, only opting out...and it will likely take you a lifetime. If you are white-bodied person like me, you must teach your white children about the water. Together, we must teach them how to swim against the current of hatred and bigotry that could easily deliver them safely to shore, while drowning their friends of color in its wake and depriving them of their full humanity. And even if our white children can swim in this hateful current, it will not keep them whole. We are all damaged by a society submerged in racial constructs and systemic oppressions.

Together we must teach our children a new way, a new kind of kinship that is actually the oldest kind of kinship, the kinship as old as Eden, the kinship expressed by my Bemba family, the kinship called forth in the language of "all my relations" that is used by many Indigenous North American tribes.

When evoked unselfconsciously by a white-bodied person like me, the notion of our shared humanity can (and has been) used to dismiss substantive differences in the experiences of diverse human beings across time and space. It has been invoked to justify assimilation of minoritized people into the dominant culture. On the flip side, it also has been used to justify appropriation of the various cultural expressions of marginalized people—food, music, art, fashion, even spiritual practices—at the same time that these very same people groups are being systematically and brutally oppressed and exploited! There it is again—the unity that covers over pain, rather than healing the wound.

But when you mean it in the Indigenous way, our shared humanity becomes the basis for one world family tied together by solidarity, not conformity. And it even goes beyond humanity, bearing witness to the relationships we share with all created beings, from the earth worms beneath us to the stars beaming over our heads. One of my favorite musicians, Jon Batiste, says it this way on his album *World Music Radio*, "We are born the same…return to that place. We are born the same…return to that place." The song is called "Worship," and I suppose that is no accident. It evokes a kind of spiritual awakening that has the potential to heal the Earth rather than destroy it.

Beloved, if we desire a better ending,
We must embrace a new beginning.
We must be baptized by new waters
that teach us
to paddle in a new direction,
upstream toward freedom,
where the blood in our veins
flows from our common human
African ancestor
and runs thicker
than any racial,
tribal,
or sectarian
tide.

Chapter 33

Endnotes on True Stories

"Shame hates it when we reach out and tell our story. It hates having words wrapped around it — it can't survive being shared."
~ Brené Brown, *The Gifts of Imperfection*

My therapist friends tell me that the ability to tell a cohesive narrative about our own lives is a key to unlocking mental health and wellbeing. So this is my story. This is a true story. It may not be the whole truth, but it is *my* truth, and that is enough truth for one story. The other characters herein, the real people involved, may have their own true stories to tell. At points, their truths may be different from my own. And that is okay.

Though the telling of this story has involved the naming of harms done, there are no villains here, only wounded people stumbling and straining toward lives worth living and stories worth telling. There is so much pain in these pages, and yet my life has not all been suffering. I know that some will question the choices I have made about which stories to tell about my own life, and which to leave by the wayside. Where are all the anecdotes about joy, vignettes about happy memories and the good things life has given you? Where are all the ways my parents excelled at parenting, for instance? Dear Reader, I assure you that those stories are there, racing across the film reel in my mind's eye and in the tranquility of my heart. But it is one of the uncomfortable mysteries of life that our episodes of pain, suffering, and vulnerability often have the most to teach us, if we can be attentive to the lessons.

It is also true that I have chosen the particular stories herein because these are the ones that had not yet seen the light of day, that had not yet been sterilized by the sun. These stories have been shrouded in shame and finally are being set free. I have been carrying them too long. I tell them now to the world in an act of deep regard for self, in an act of generous self-love, that I might lay my own worthy version of the story on the altar of Truth.

Isn't that the best any of us can do? To tell the truth as we understand it, first to ourselves and then to each other. And then to stay open to other truths...until one day the telling of our truths finally does set us all free.

May it be so. Amen.

Acknowledgments

To my writing coach, author and teacher Charlotte Gulick: This book probably wouldn't exist without your presence in my life! You made me believe I could write a book, and you've helped me make it a good one. Deep gratitude to you for every push, prod, question, edit, and word of encouragement you have offered me for over seven years now.

To the members of my 2017 Collegeville Institute Seminar Cohort at Austin Presbyterian Theological Seminary, where the idea for this memoir was born: Thank you for helping me feel like a real writer among writers. To Keith Ray and Paul Lutter, in particular, thank you for the ways you inspire me with the lives you lead and the meaning you make from them.

To my parents, thank you for all the hard work, sacrifice, and love you invested to give me three essential building blocks for a generative life: Access to quality healthcare, a really good education, and the tools to cultivate my own spirituality. I love you.

To my older sister, Trish, when I was small and struggling with debilitating insecurities and self-doubt, you taught me about confidence. I hope you haven't forgotten that your boldness is a gift.

To Ellis, I hope that one day the distance between us can be narrowed by the triumph of laughter over grievance.

To the Rev. Dr. Angela Yarber and Tehom Center Publishing: Thank you, thank you, thank you for making my publishing dream come true, and thank you for all the ways you are amplifying voices that need to be heard.